BOTH S
THE FENCE

BOTH SIDES OF
THE FENCE

A Life in League & Union

Bev Risman

Scratching Shed Publishing Ltd

Typeset in Warnock Pro Semi Bold and Palatino
Printed and bound in the United Kingdom by
Latimer Trend & Company Ltd,
Estover Road, Plymouth, PL6 7PY

To my family, sons Martin, John and Michael, and my brother John and their families.

And to my dearest wife Ann, who has supported me through 60 years of rugby and been vital in the production of this book.

Contents

Acknowledgements

My thanks to Lord (Melvyn) Bragg for his generous foreword and for sharing his own early experiences of rugby in West Cumberland.

I am indebted to the following for their comments, reminiscences and advice; Ronnie Dawson, Ray French, David Hinchliffe, Lionel Hurst, Richard Lewis, David Oxley, John Risman, Alan Smith, Ken Scotland, Graeme Thompson, the late Joe Warham and Niel Wood

The books by Dave Hadfield, Julian Harrison, Peter Lush and Dave Farrar have been of particular relevance in covering the development of student rugby league, the Rugby League Conference and the Fulham and London Broncos clubs.

Jack Bainbridge and the editorial staff of the *Leigh Journal* enabled me to recall the details of my career there and Raymond Fletcher, John Ledger and Arthur Haddock of the *Yorkshire Post* and *Yorkshire Evening Post* helped me to research my career at Leeds by providing access to the newspapers archives.

Professor Tony Collins, Martyn Sadler and editor Phil Caplan have given me the benefit of their experience, and our friends and colleagues in the rugby world including Barbara and Derek Hallas and Ron and Gladys Cowan have proffered advice and shared so many rugby experiences.

Our friends Jenny and Mike Senior have also supplied invaluable assistance on the finer points of writing a book.

Foreword

Lord Melvyn Bragg

I first met Bev Risman on the rugby field. It could be my greatest claim to fame.

It was on a muddy pitch at Cockermouth Grammar School in the 1950s, which Bev attended. I was playing for Wigton Nelson Thomlinson Grammar School, which was about 15 miles away. I remember it vividly because we were told by our PT teacher (an ex England international) and by three of the boys in our team who had played with Bev as Under 18 English internationals that we were going to meet a genius and we had better watch out.

The pitch was a quagmire. The rain came down as if determined to make another lake in that northern part of the Lake District. Wigton had not been beaten for a couple of seasons. Cockermouth were only a moderate side but they had Bev Risman.

I hope he won't mind me saying so but we were all over them (let me here declare that I was picked because there were not many boys in the sixth form in those days, and after all this was rugby union and we needed fifteen players). But somehow or other by positioning or organising his team or by pinpoint kicking, this single player – already a legend in schools' rugby – prevented us from scoring. I think we managed a mighty draw, 0-0. Afterwards it is retrospectively moving to remember that our three internationals who had played with him for England crowded round him proudly in admiration while the rest of us stood back and hoped for a friendly nod. Yes, he was that good even then.

Our PT teacher explained a few days later that he had watched Bev very closely throughout the game (why was he not watching us?) and noticed that whenever he got the ball he seemed to have all the time in the world to work out how he would optimise the situation. He was never fazed.

That gift never left him in what can only be called an astonishing career. He got eight caps for the full England side, and was with the British Lions in Australia and New Zealand in 1959. In 1961 he turned professional and joined Leigh rugby league club. That was a very bold act in those days. Snobbery more or less everywhere in England then and certainly in rugby it was thicker than double cream and gentlemen did not play rugby league.

Well Bev Risman did and in 1967 he was awarded "Best & Fairest Player in the League" by rugby league writers – the first gentleman of the professional sport. In that year and the two subsequent years he was also the leading goal kicker in rugby league. He was never less than a gentleman and never less than a great rugby player.

In rugby league he captained the British Lions tour to Australia in 1968 and when playing for Leeds between 1967 and 1970 he led them to the Rugby League Championship Final and the top of the league for four consecutive years. He had moved to a game most rugby union players feared as being too tough to play – and he had triumphed in it.

You could say that some of it was inherited. His father, Gus, was one of the all-time great international players. He was elected to the Rugby League Hall of Fame. He managed and played for Workington Town which is a 50-minute bus ride from Wigton. What we did in those heady days of rugby league in West Cumbria in the early 1950s was to play for our school in the morning , jump on a bus and go to Workington to see what was one of the finest rugby league teams in the country.

My father had a pub then in Wigton, and one of the Draymen was Billy Ivison. He and a chap called Stan used to deliver the barrels and crates of beer. I remember several times (it must have been out of season or in the holidays) watching it all as Stan roped up the barrels at the front of the pub and eased them down the ramp into the cellar where Billy would take them and put them on built-up railway sleepers waiting to settle before they were tapped by my father.

Billy got me the signatures of all the Workington Team. He was as gentle mannered a man as you could hope to meet. He was not particularly tall but very broad and amazingly light on his feet. They would say that he could hold a rugby ball up ended on the tip of his index finger and dodge his way through the other team! He too played for Great Britain.

Rugby league was the hard man's game, the game that miners played when they came up from a morning shift, the game where men needed to be paid for their training time and games. Just like their peers in the footballing towns and cities. But what was sauce for the soccer goose was not in those days sauce for the rugby union gander. Those who played rugby league were thought to be, well, below the salt, i.e. working class. Rugby union, everybody then knew, was an upper class game despite the fact that boys from all backgrounds took it up.

So Bev was not only a gentleman hero, he also became something of a model and leader for those who wanted or needed to be paid for their Saturday sport, which was then watched by many thousands in Workington Town.

Tom Keneally, the Australian novelist who won the Booker Prize for *Schindler's Ark*, is a passionate fan of rugby league and never ceases to express gratitude to me (!) simply because I come from the North of England where rugby league was invented. It sailed over to Australia, passing through Europe along the way. It is a marvellous game, fast, unfussy, and I believe that Bev has some strong points to make about the two codes.

His has been a life of major achievement, not only with rugby but in tennis (he was Under 18 junior champion for Cumberland & Westmoreland for whom he also played cricket). He has been a Physical Education teacher in schools and universities. Happily married to Ann, three boys, all of whom play rugby, as do their sons!

Throughout it all though, I keep seeing the calm watchful face and the wholly deceptive unhurried style of that brilliant adolescent Cumbrian lad holding at bay almost single-handedly a rampant team.

Lord Melvyn Bragg

A National Dilemma

1

Some days stand out all your life. You occasionally replay them in your mind, crystal clear, because significant, life-changing decisions were made.

The first for me came in November 1958. It was my 21st birthday and I had just received an invitation to play in the first Wales rugby union trial at Pontypool. Good news you may think. The only problem was that I was born in Salford, Lancashire and had lived all my life in the north of England.

I'd often been on holiday to South Wales and, on several occasions, taken part in rugby tours there. The offer from the Welsh came principally because my father, Gus, was one of the icons of rugby league. He was born in the Principality of Latvian parents, who had settled in Wales at the beginning of the twentieth century.

John Reason, one of the most prominent rugby union journalists at the time, clearly identified my dilemma.

"If he plays in the Welsh trial he will not be considered by England. But if he turns down the invitation and subsequently plays in an England trial, he could still win a Welsh cap."

What a farce! Nowadays, it's much more open, you can qualify by birth, ancestry or residence, creating a situation which allows possible movement of players from one country to another almost at will.

Not for the first or last time, I found myself on both sides of the fence.

I'd always regarded myself as English but the national selectors had given no indication that I figured in their plans despite press speculation.

If I went to the Valleys and was a miserable failure, the likelihood was that any hopes of an international career would be over before it began.

On the other hand, the great Cliff Morgan had just retired and Wales were looking for a new fly-half. It could just be my chance.

I was in my third season of senior rugby union having captained the England Schools U18s. I'd played for Cumberland and Westmorland in my first season and Lancashire in my second- having moved back to live there.

After some success in the representative schools matches, I was being tipped in the press as a potential full international.

Up to that point, I'd played mostly union but had also turned out now and then in junior rugby league competitions.

I loved it and in fact, my dream was to emulate my father and become a professional player, I had grown up in the full spotlight of his fame and renown in West Cumberland.

Our life as a family had revolved around rugby league in Workington where Dad was truly revered.

As post-war player/manager of fledgling Workington Town, he had taken the club to Championship and Challenge Cup glory and in his own way had helped Cumberland to recover from the ravages of post-war austerity and recession.

He gave the area something to be proud of and his position on the rugby league statue at Wembley is testimony to the esteem in which he was held in the sport.

Wales or England considerations apart, I was on the horns of another dilemma at the time, should I stay in union or go to my first love, league.

This was at the height of the dark days of rugby apartheid. When I chatted about the situation to my rugby playing friends, they were not slow to remind me that once a union player even set foot in league territory, he would be banned for life from playing, coaching, serving on a committee or even socialising within the 15-man game – how draconian it all seems now.

My father deliberately kept me away from the league scouts who by this time were making their interest known.

He acted as my minder, adviser and unofficial agent and in the end his counsel prevailed.

I was hoping to go to university in Manchester to study Geology and had been awarded a county major scholarship from Cumberland.

Life as a student and signed on rugby player would not mix in those days and Dad advised me strongly to wait and at least start mapping out a career away from sport as an insurance for later life.

He also dangled the carrot that if I did make the grade in union, I would subsequently receive a much higher signing on fee as and when the chance came to cross over.

After I left Cockermouth Grammar school, full of my exploits for Cumberland and Westmorland and England Schools, my first senior match, at the age of 18, was for a North of England Select XV versus South of Scotland.

The team was full of players with lots of representative experience such as Harry Scott (England) Ken Jones and Alan Ashcroft (England and British Lions) and I was told I'd gone okay.

An unofficial trial match for Cumberland and Westmorland against The Army followed back at Cockermouth, where I was opposed to my old friend Ken Scotland who went on to represent Scotland and the British Lions.

Things couldn't have been going better, it appeared and I played a couple of games for Manchester University before my first county championship match in the derby against Northumberland.

We lost and I received what I thought was an innocuous wrist injury. I completed the game but it stiffened up when I got back.

Knowing that I was due to play in a university fixture on the following Wednesday, I went to hospital straightaway and was met by Duncan Cranna, a surgeon who also happened to be president of the university rugby club.

He sent me for a precautionary X-ray which found that I had broken my scaphoid, a delicate bone in the wrist.

I was threatened with arthritis if I didn't have it treated so it was immediately put in plaster and stayed that way for four months, meaning I missed virtually the whole of my first season.

It is not an exaggeration to say that I was devastated. Worse still, the bone refused to heal and I was not able to train, never mind play.

From being a potential England trialist, I immediately became a forgotten man and as one plaster cast was replaced by another, I felt sure that my aspirations were in ruins before they had even begun.

I was new to learning how to cope with the serious injuries that plague all rugby players at some time or other.

My only previous setbacks had been stitches in the back of my leg after being kicked by a lad wearing clogs in an U16s rugby league cup match, and having a bump the size of an egg on my forehead when I was hit by a cricket ball while playing wicketkeeper for the school team.

The upshot of this enforced idleness was a need to plan what to do with my spare time. Throwing myself into my studies was not really an option as, although I thoroughly enjoyed the subject, I saw myself as a sportsman first and foremost.

My grandmother had taught me how to play cards for matchsticks so I spent much of my time gambling away my student grant playing poker, blackjack and bridge and eventually became quite good, which stood me in good stead on various away trips and rugby tours.

There was snooker, billiards and table tennis learned at the Cockermouth Conservative Club but I drifted aimlessly, getting more and more frustrated thinking about the opportunities I was missing and watching others achieving the successes I had hoped for.

There was, however, one saving grace. Because the injury did not affect my appetite which was and still is immense, I grew and put on two stones which took me to an ideal playing weight.

I was now a 5' 8" barrel and 13 stone. I'd not lost any pace but gained muscle and was subsequently able to stand up to the inherent hard knocks.

I only ever lost half a stone after that and stayed at my fighting weight for the next ten years.

In March 1957, after five months out, the plaster came off for the final time and the bone had healed at last.

I could have cried, first with happiness and secondly with dismay when I looked at the poor shrivelled limb covered with dead skin.

I was assured that it would recover quickly with the right rehabilitation and was thrilled to be running about the rugby field again.

Fortunately it coincided with the end-of-season tour the university had organised, a three match trip to France, based at Terrasson.

It was probably not the best environment to make a comeback. We were treated like royalty by the rugby-mad French and showered with food and wine galore.

But it was a wonderful first experience of going abroad to play.

Forced to Move

2

I loved everything about Cumberland but, out of the blue, in July 1954, after years of outstanding success at Workington, my father resigned from his job at Borough Park.

His amazing and record-breaking career is recounted in his autobiography *Rugby Renegade*. In it he gives his version of what happened when the directors signed a replacement for him without consultation whilst we were on holiday.

For the record, Dad made Town arguably the best club in the game after only five years in existence. He put Workington on the rugby map.

He was then, and still is, the oldest player ever to appear in a Challenge Cup final at Wembley at nearly 42.

As news went round of his departure, there was uproar and my father's pride was terribly shaken after all he had done for the club. So we moved back to Lancashire, a place I felt no affinity with despite being born there.

Dad was on the outer and although he still had his sports shop in Workington, rugby was in his blood and he still felt that there was much for him to do in the game.

Even at the age of 43 he was still superbly fit and when Batley asked him to play for them, he didn't hesitate.

It was a short-term option as he was looking for a manager's job and there were overtures from his old club Salford, who were struggling at the time.

He was appointed there in February 1955 and started another phase in his illustrious career.

Rugby-wise, even though I was still eligible for Cumberland and Westmorland, our move to Manchester meant a transfer of allegiance to the Red Rose county, despite some reluctance on my part.

It was basically back to square one in what was, effectively, my first full senior season in 1957-8.

Any possible delusions of grandeur had long gone and I realised, ruefully, that I had to take a much more pragmatic approach to working my way up the ranks again.

All thoughts of International caps were forgotten as I struggled to come to terms with reality.

Having been so long out of the game, I began to doubt my abilities and the way selection operated in those days did not help.

Then, any choices for county or international teams were made as a result of countless trial matches.

Lancashire had a formidable reputation with, invariably, a number of internationals in their team.

When I became eligible, Eric Evans was the current England captain at hooker, Reg Higgins and Alan Ashcroft in the back row, Martin Regan at fly-half and Reg Bazley on the wing were outstanding backs.

In the early part of season, I played a number of

games for Manchester as well as the university and the North of England select, so I had the opportunity to show what I could do in the local arena.

For me, all trials are a shambles. None of the players really know each other, there is no time to practice together and continuous chopping and changing throughout the games.

If you were on the weaker side you had little chance of selection, regulars tended to be pencilled in immediately and had to have nightmare performances not to be selected.

Often it was matter of who you knew, or who knew you.

In the end I did get selected for Lancashire although there were still some doubters in the press, who always seemed to have a big say in the final choice.

I played in every match that I could that season, combining regular appearances for Manchester University on Saturdays and Wednesdays, unofficial representative matches, Sunday charity games, pre-season, Christmas and Easter tours and representing Lancashire.

With the relief of finally being back out there, I enjoyed every one of them.

At last I felt at home in senior rugby even as a relative youngster and was in my element travelling all over the country with little time for training and certainly none for studies.

As an amateur you had so much more freedom as to who you turned out for and how often you played in those times.

The County Championship was regarded as the selectors' benchmark for the internationals.

Playing for your club was important but there were no leagues and each English club's fixture list was made up of a series of friendlies and traditional games which remained basically the same every season.

In the North, the county matches had added meaning. Lancashire were grouped with Cheshire, Cumberland and Westmorland, Durham, Northumberland and Yorkshire and the highlight of the season was the annual Roses match.

The Championship, which ended up in a final at Twickenham, was essentially the first stage of selection for international honours and provided a shop window, alongside the anachronism that was the annual varsity match between the universities of Oxford and Cambridge.

At one time the land management course at Cambridge was almost full of 'students' with great rugby pedigrees.

My debut for Lancashire was against Cheshire at Blundellsands, the home of Waterloo, and I was subjected to the infamous Eric Evans hair dryer treatment in the changing room before the match started.

His approach was totally alien to me as I always tried to keep calm and focussed before a game and although I went through the motions of getting hyped up and angry, the head-banging style never really appealed to me.

I always went through my own warm up and stretching ritual and preferred a large mouthful of sherry to get my adrenalin going, a tip inherited from Dad.

Nevertheless, something obviously worked, we won 18-9, future international full-back John Wilcox had an outstanding game and I felt I had made a sound start.

Two more narrow wins followed against Durham and Northumberland and, suddenly, we were favourites for the Northern Championship.

Memorable in the match against Durham was the exceptional kicking of Mike Weston, my opponent at fly-half, who was putting the ball almost into orbit, torturing anyone who was brave enough to get underneath it.

We thrashed my old county Cumberland and Westmorland 34-nil but it was a rather sensitive game for me because, although it was my best performance, I still felt like a deserter.

That meant we only had to draw against Yorkshire at Otley to get to the semi-finals for the first time for a while.

They had a formidable side particularly in the backs with British Lions Geoff Butterfield and Frank Sykes, England's Peter Thompson and experienced half-backs Wynn and Shuttleworth. Things looked grim when we lost our scrum half Arthur Crick early on – there were no replacements in those days – but we were still in contention with the strong wind at our backs in the second half.

Much against my nature, I spent the whole time hoofing the ball down field and we kept Yorkshire penned in their own half with frantic defending, and a sensational backs-to-the-wall 11-all draw earned us a trip to Cornwall in the semis.

I had now re-established myself. I was getting some reasonable write-ups but no contact had been made from either Wales or England and my name did not appear in any of the trials teams announced in December.

Manchester University had put together a useful side, there were national championships and in the north we also had a triangular competition for the Christie Shield against Leeds and Liverpool.

University rugby was probably the most enjoyable I played at 15-a-side because it was full of free flowing and adventurous play.

When facing club sides we had no chance of keeping the ball tight with their more experienced and battle hardened forwards, so it was a matter of trying to run them off their feet from the start.

It was often exhilarating, although occasionally we had to take a physical pummelling.

Great friendships made in my four years at university have lasted a lifetime. I am still in touch with my fellow captains Dave Parker and Geoff Stringer and keep in contact with scrum-half partner, Welshman Terry Humphries who kept me out of trouble on the field and got me into it off it.

It was very easy to live day by day and just think from one match to the next, which I was prone to do.

I continued to live in Hulme Hall of Residence at the university but home was now much more accessible and I was able to spend more time with my mother and father and younger brother John who was now in his teens.

They were able to come to watch me and Dad became a regular visitor to our home matches at Fallowfield.

Despite all the rugby distractions, studies were critically important.

There was no full-time paid professional rugby in those days and I learned a very early lesson when I failed one of my exams in chemistry, which was an integral part of the geology degree in my first year.

I didn't realise the significance of extra study until it was too late and was really panicking when I had to re-sit my exam in September under the threat of a repeat year or even being kicked off the course.

It was a terrible paper, I found it really difficult and was in turmoil for several days waiting for the results wondering if I had ruined my potential life path.

I passed, although it must have been by the skin of my teeth, and swore that I would never neglect my studies again.

I never missed another lecture or practical – even after a Wednesday afternoon game and obligatory social session afterwards – and nor failed another exam.

Mum and Dad were a great influence at this time as the rugby became very demanding and they were a continuous source of encouragement and guidance, helping me to keep a happy medium between studies and sport.

Mum took care of the domestics, doing my washing and providing food hampers and well as warning me all the time about the pitfalls of booze and women.

Dad kept me on the straight and narrow with my sport, giving me praise when merited and lots of sound advice to ensure that I didn't get ahead of myself.

I was also very fortunate in having a steady girlfriend. Ann and I were at school together and had been going out for over a year before university.

I had admired her from afar for a long while particularly on the hockey field, netball and tennis courts and the athletics track. She was an outstanding sportswoman but also brilliant academically. There was only one difficulty, I was only four foot six and she was five feet eight.

I stuck to girls my own size for a while but with the help of a sudden growth spurt I almost caught up with her and had the courage to ask her out.

We have been together ever since, only apart for two years at different universities and six months when I was away on tour with the British Lions in 1959.

Ann was the top scholar in Cumberland in our 'A' level year and was destined for Cambridge.

Fortunately for me she chose Manchester straight away rather than stay on at school for another year to get advanced Latin, which was necessary in those days for Oxbridge entrance.

We got married immediately after university and Ann eventually went on to become principal of Richmond Adult College in West London, receiving recognition for her work by the awarding of an OBE in 1999.

During 1957-58, Ann and I were beginning to mix with a new circle of friends in addition to those we had made during our schooldays; Maurice Watson and Dinah Large and one of our best companions, Brian Goodfellow and his partner Frances Greggains.

Maurice and Brian were both rugby players and we were all in the same hall of residence, as was Mike Senior, whose girlfriend Jenny shared Ann's. The girls immediately hit it off together.

We still visit each other often and have had many wonderful holidays together. Mike, who read history, is an expert on World War I and has published several books on the subject.

Geoff Stringer started off as one of my team mates and drinking partners at Manchester. He refers to himself as the first of the ball-handling prop forwards in rugby union and used to amaze everyone with his pace and dextrous skills. I'm sure that he could have gone on to greater things had selectors recognised that it was useful for front-rowers to use their brains as well as their brawn.

Geoff played for Wasps and Blackheath when he moved south to establish a very successful career as a lawyer.

Apart from my father, the other person who influenced my sporting career more than anyone else was my friend from junior school days, Frank Burns.

From the age of 10 when we first met we had only one interest, sport. We were both fanatical competitors and for ten years or so knocked hell out of each other playing every conceivable game you could imagine.

Harris Park in Cockermouth was the venue for many of our contests.

There was bowls, putting and marathon tennis matches. Swimming races in the river Cocker and kicking contests with the rugby ball - often all in one day.

Then back to our house to play darts, snooker, cards, monopoly and even the occasional boxing bout under strict rules from my dad.

Frank and I used to run around the golf course at Embleton. Dad played there every Sunday morning and Frank and I would get in three games of snooker in the club house before his four-ball finished.

Although we occasionally had a heated confrontation over a controversial decision, most of our games were fought out in a good spirit and, even at such an early age, they taught us to deal with winning and losing.

After training as an engineer while I was at university, Frank became a professional soldier rising to the rank of lieutenant colonel in the REME Army Air Corps and despite being posted to all parts of the world, he continued to pursue and champion sport.

He represented the Army at tennis, golf and rugby and was to have been our best man in 1961 but was called up to serve in Aden.

Just after the Universities Athletic Union Christmas tour in 1957-8 there were a number of key matches.

English Universities beat Scottish Universities 6-3 and our points were two tries scored by a Welshman, W.G.D. Morgan who went on to play for England and eventually reached the exalted heights of president of the RFU.

Also on our team were future internationals, Englishmen Stan Purdy and Brian Whiteman and Alan Pask from Wales.

For the UAU against the RAF I came up against, arguably, the most enigmatic performer of all in David Onllwyn 'Onkers' Brace.

He became renowned for his incredibly unorthodox methods, playing sevens-style rugby in a 15-a-side environment.

A look at the rest of the RAF back line that season shows the quality available – Frank Carlton (Wigan rugby league), Malcolm Price (Wales and British Lions), Mike Wade (England), Roy Sandstrom (GB athlete) and my immediate opponent, fly-half Graham Paul (Cornwall RFU and future Hull Kingston Rover). But we managed to contain them and eventually won 21-5.

My greatest thrill that season was selection for North West Counties against the touring Australians in February 1958, my first experience on the senior international scene.

It meant little that the Wallabies were not at their strongest, having already lost against Wales 9-3 and Ireland 9-6, they were still formidable opposition for a scratch side that had virtually no preparation time.

Prominent in their ranks were prop and captain Bob Davidson, celebrated front-rower Nick Shehadie, flying winger Ken Donald and talented fly-half Arthur Summons.

The match was played at Waterloo in atrocious conditions with the pitch heavy thanks to snow and a gale force wind.

It was basically our defence against their attack and to the Australians' great credit, they persisted in playing running rugby for the whole match.

We were on the back foot for most of the game and I was confined to a defensive kicking game while Summons treated the crowd to an exhilarating exhibition of passing and running.

That was a great lesson for me and I resolved to try to emulate him and expand my repertoire regardless.

We achieved a famous 6-3 victory and paid no heed to the fact that the tourists ended with one of the worst playing records and were said to be the dirtiest team to come to the British Isles, although there was no evidence of foul play in this encounter.

A week later it was the County Championship semi-final against Cornwall and we travelled to what seemed like end of the world to face them at Redruth.

Talk about intimidation, the fans filled every corner of the famous sloping ground. I had heard of the fervent Cornishmen by reputation and although we were regarded as marginal favourites, everything changed in that environment.

Cornwall played above themselves, roared on by their supporters and we failed to really do ourselves justice and lost 14-8.

It was the most disappointing result of my career to date but the momentous season was only half way through, despite playing over thirty matches by then.

As it drew to a close, I played in a centenary celebration for Liverpool-Manchester against Richmond-Blackheath at Liverpool's famous Aigburth ground.

It was Barbarian type rugby, free-flowing and expansive, and one of the most enjoyable games I have ever played in, with great personalities on both sides.

In the Shadow of a Legend

3

In 1936, a year before my arrival, my father had established himself as one of the all-time rugby league greats, having been an integral part of the Great Britain Lions who toured Australia down under.

After losing the First Test convincingly in Australia, the Lions came back to win the series, with Dad taking over as captain from Jim Brough for the deciding encounter in Sydney and the two victories against New Zealand.

He returned home to skipper all-conquering Salford along with his team mates on the tour, Alan Edwards, Barney Hudson, Emlyn Jenkins and Billy Watkins, all of them backs.

The Red Devils, as they were christened on an historic tour that helped to help establish the sport in France, won trophies galore in the 1930s including three championships and a Challenge Cup victory at Wembley against Barrow in 1938.

I used to go to matches from soon after being born but

with the onset of the Second World War, sport was put into mothballs and that great Salford era came to an abrupt end.

In his autobiography my father said nothing about his military service, few soldiers do.

He served in the Physical Training Corps and had front line experience in the Military Police and the Paratroop Regiment and was posted home and abroad.

My mother and I were able to travel with him to places like Northallerton, Mitchett and Aldershot and, whenever he was able, a ball would come out and he would help me develop the essential skills.

He spent some time overseas, especially in Algiers, but whenever he was back in England he was sought after to play rugby league in one-off matches, usually arranged by Eddie Waring at Dewsbury, or rugby union representing the Armed Forces or Welsh Services made up from a mixture of stars from both codes.

All previous animosity and regulation was relaxed or abandoned during the combat.

Aged four or five, I can remember practising my place kicking with a full sized ball in our back garden both when my father was at home and on my own.

My first attempts at playing were in 30-a-side matches on the recreation ground cinders on Langworthy Road when I was at Seedley Junior School, Salford.

We played with a big ball made up of a knotted scarf, and anyone between the ages of seven and 13 would take part.

I still have a lasting impression of air raid sirens and shelters and my grandad, an air raid warden, coming round to check we were alright, all interspersed with happy days at school where I was in the same class as now world-renowned actor Albert Finney.

My rugby career and, in fact, my life was seriously threatened when, at the age of seven, I was carted off to Salford Royal Infirmary in an ambulance having contracted a very serious kidney infection, at the same time as a severe dose of measles, which was rife at the time.

I was kept in hospital for some time and my mother was told I could have become permanently disabled.

In 1946, when I was nine, we moved to Cumberland when my father took charge of Workington Town.

Our house in Cockermouth backed on to the beautiful Harris Park and every morning, without fail, Dad would start the day with his first training session there.

I went with him as often as I could, although there was some reluctance at six o'clock in the morning, especially in the depths of winter.

He was an iron man as far as his training was concerned.

We never went without a rugby ball and spent the time practising handling and kicking skills as well as running, sprinting, sidestepping and swerving - I loved it!

For a change we sometimes went for an early morning dip in the freezing River Cocker when the weather was suitable.

My friends now don't believe me when I describe this Spartan upbringing but anyone who knew my father would recognise it, and in our family he was always held up as an example of how a serious player should behave.

In the summer, all the towns and villages in the area held sports meetings which included athletics, cycling, fell racing, and the championships of Cumberland and Westmorland wrestling.

My father would enter me for the 100 yards handicap sprints for 8-16 year olds.

I was only nine or ten at the time but was quite quick and, with a good start on the older boys, managed to pick up a few prizes including watches, barometers, a table-tennis set and even a bicycle.

It was all taken very seriously, especially amongst the parents, who used to try and wangle the handicaps and Dad was very quick to cotton on.

In my first-ever race in the Cockermouth and District Primary School Sports, I was up against a lad called John Coan in my heat.

He turned up in all the gear, which included a brand new pair of running spikes.

I was wearing my standard issue Dunlop Blue Flash gym shoes and he beat me easily on the slippery grass but I qualified for the next round and eventually the final.

Not to be outdone, Dad searched around and managed to get hold of a pair of spikes which he insisted that I wore in the final.

I just pipped John Coan in it and at the same time learned a good lesson about having the right equipment and playing the system.

Dad was something of a gentle persuader, convincing me of the value of exercise and training and I was always a willing workhorse.

My first games of rugby were at Fairfield Junior School where we had a big sloping field at the back that everyone gathered on at lunchtime.

Forget football, rugby touch or touch and pass were the order of the day and Frank Burns, Eddie Thomas and I took on the rest of the class, usually about twenty of them.

Our only advantage was that we played downhill.

The ball was the usual knotted scarf and the three of us side stepped, swerved, ducked and dummied our way through the matches hotly pursued by the rest, it worked wonders for my evasive skills.

My brother John fondly remembers those early years. "Cockermouth was a wonderful place," he says.

"The Risman family lived there from just after the end of World War two until the mid-1950s. Our house was on Fern Bank next to Harris Park and the river Cocker. I was an avid fisherman and brought home trout and the occasional salmon, which my mother and father loved.

"We had a full family life and Bev and I grew up as real country boys with good friends and few problems."

I graduated to Cockermouth Grammar School via the 11 plus exam but we had no proper rugby matches other than in games lessons, until the first inter-school matches began at U15 level.

Regardless, touch rugby continued in the school yard with often several matches often going on in the same playground area.

A lot of the boys and girls were fans of my father's team and went to watch the Workington matches on a Saturday afternoon.

I was in a privileged position and Dad took me with him to most Saturday home games at Borough Park.

Every time he played, he went through his 'Risman ritual' – raw eggs and sherry and a ten-minute catnap.

Only then would we set off to be at the club, well before the other players arrived.

I was allowed to go into the changing room and used to help kit man John Wilson put out the jerseys, shorts, socks, jock straps, boots and towels and, if I was lucky, would borrow a couple of balls and go out onto the pitch before the crowds were let in, to race about trying to fulfil my fantasies of playing for Town.

When the players began to arrive, I was able to listen to their banter and pick up a few Australian swearwords from the likes of Tony Paskins and Johnny Mudge, whilst the broad-accented Cumbrian props Jimmy Waring and Jimmy Hayton retaliated in kind.

My father turned a deaf ear to all that.

As they started to get changed, I drifted into the narrow corridor next to the dressing rooms and found ways and means of flinging the ball about until kick-off time approached.

Once it did, I'd try to sneak into the dug-out or go behind the posts at the river end to watch the match with thousands of supporters packing the terraces.

Although forced to play union at school as that was all there was, all my heroes were in rugby league.

I knew the names and positions of every one of the Workington team and the reserves and legendary players of the other teams such as Eric Batten, Jack Kitching, Ernest Ward, Willie Horne, Ken Gee, Joe Egan, Frank Whitcombe, Trevor Foster and Ike Owens. Later there was Jimmy Ledgard, Ernie Ashcroft, Dicky Williams, Tommy Bradshaw and the two Harrys – Murphy and Street.

Even when I started playing school's representative rugby union, I continued to avidly watch the likes of Gerry Helme, Alan Prescott, Dave Valentine, Phil Jackson, Ken Traill and even players who I eventually played against when I turned professional; Billy Boston, Lewis Jones, Dougie Greenall and Geoff Gunney.

The support for Workington was fanatical and at school we used to play our matches on a Saturday morning and then rush off to catch one of the convoy of double-decker buses which left Cockermouth Main Street to ferry the crowd to the ground.

Although it was a relatively small co-ed school, Cockermouth Grammar had a very strong and successful rugby union pedigree.

We had teams at U15 and senior U18 level playing against most other schools in Cumberland and Westmorland.

At age 13 and eligible for the 15's, my predicament was that I was so small.

I was initially quite quick but others rapidly overtook me, my growth spurt failed to materialise and I still had to wear short trousers.

There was only one position that I could play and that was scrum-half but for three years I had to rely on my wits and skill to avoid being hammered.

All my early days of touch rugby stood me in good stead and I was chosen for the county U15 side two years running.

I played well and was picked to represent the North of England against the Midlands in the trials for the youth international team.

We won the match convincingly and I had received good reports so I obviously hoped to be chosen.

It didn't happen.

My lack of stature had never been mentioned as a problem in the past but it appeared that the selectors decided that I was too small and I was left out of the final trial.

I was devastated to be left out especially because it hadn't been on ability.

I hated selectors for a while but at long last started to thicken out and, from being a four-foot-six weakling eventually grew to five feet eight on tiptoe by the time I was 17, and played for England Schools U18s for two years at fly-half.

During my schooldays, the only opportunity I had to

play league was in an U16 junior competition organised by the Cumberland Amateur Rugby League, and several of us from Cockermouth opted to join the Maryport side

We played a match against pretty poor opposition, including one lad who obviously had very little idea of the rules. He attempted to tackle me by scything me down feet first as in soccer.

I felt an instant stabbing pain and looked in horror at the back of my calf, seeing that it had been gouged open and was bleeding profusely – and my best rugby socks had been torn!

Glaring at the assailant, I noticed for the first time that he was actually wearing metal clogs instead of boots.

There was no checking of footwear beforehand at this level in those days and as a result I needed several stitches.

The wound did eventually heal but the important thing was that we went on to win the trophy but it was no more rugby league for me after that for quite a while.

* * * * * *

I couldn't have wished for a more enjoyable and successful first full season in the senior union ranks.

Ann and I had a very busy social life but my rugby commitments became more intense and she had her own sporting commitments as well as developing her academic career.

Our relationship had matured despite the many distractions even though I became very jealous and possessive about her going out and socialising when I was away playing rugby.

But I like to think we were always there for each other when it really mattered and it must have worked.

I felt much happier about combining my studies and sporting commitments and when I was asked to be captain of the university team, had no hesitation in accepting and was really looking forward to the extra responsibility.

Towards the end of April 1958, Lancashire agreed to play Ulster in a special memorial match for Eric Allen, a stalwart Irish prop forward who died on New Year's Day as a result of a severe injury received in a collapsed scrum.

We travelled to Belfast to play against a star studded XV and there was a great turnout to recognise the sterling service that Eric had given to the game in his native land.

In such circumstances the match seemed incidental but, nonetheless, was taken very seriously by all concerned.

We put on a magnificent display scoring 14 tries in a 58-3 victory against a team containing 10 internationals.

From a personal point of view it was an honour to be able to lock horns with Jack Kyle, one of the all-time great fly-halves who was just coming to the end of a long and glittering career.

He was a great man on and off the field and devoted his career after rugby in the medical profession to a lifetime of caring for the underprivileged in Africa.

He became one of my heroes and I regard myself as fortunate to have got to know him well as a friend in our later years.

That summer seemed to fly by. I played a bit of tennis and golf and in no time the next season was upon me.

It was about this time that people, inevitably, started to compare me more and more with my father, some older ones often unfavourably.

Dad's stellar career had now come to an end and those jibes worried me for a while but I soon realised that there was no real similarity at this stage.

I used such comments as a spur and one positive it did have was that my name was continually being brought into the spotlight.

I'm certain that was why I was given the opportunity to continually prove myself in various representative teams and touring parties.

A good example was when I was asked to join the prestigious Ranji Walker's tour of South Wales in early September.

In many people's eyes, this was second only to the Barbarians and the composite team played against the cream of Principality talent.

South Wales was a hotbed and at the time it was recognised as a true spiritual home of union, where careers could be made or ruined.

If there is one match that I am convinced rocketed me to prominence, it was the one against Cardiff, when I was paired at half back with 'Onkers' Brace.

He was at his mercurial best, we seemed to hit it off immediately and completely overshadowed Cardiff's international half backs, Ken Richards and Lloyd Williams, to spearhead a famous 17-5 victory.

I scored two tries and I swear that when I crossed for the first, every single Cardiff player had their eyes on Brace as he careered across the field throwing dummies right and left, before nonchalantly slipping a reverse pass to me to stroll through a huge gap to touchdown between the posts.

He was already a seasoned international, having played in all four matches for Wales in 1956, had skippered them twice and gained nine caps in all but it appears that the selectors were never quite convinced about him and mostly preferred Lloyd Williams to the little genius.

I didn't see Onllwyn for years after that but I'll always

be eternally grateful to him because I believe that he was one of the main factors behind my eventual international selection.

After the tour, in which I scored tries in all four games, I returned to my university commitments and the county games with Lancashire.

I had been getting some good write ups and although I had previously represented England at schools and university level, out of the blue when I was invited to play in the first Welsh trial because Dad had been born in Cardiff.

There was much talk about who would be Cliff Morgan's successor. The two most likely candidates were Aberavon's Cliff Ashton and Ken Richards of Cardiff so my call-up came as a great shock.

I was not short of advice from all sides.

Dad said he would not influence my decision, all my many Welsh friends told me I had to wear the red and naturally the ones with English heritage were in no doubt I should wait for their call.

Although it was a great temptation to take the Welsh opportunity, deep down I knew that there was only one correct decision.

I was English and always would be and I would just have to take my chance and hope that the England selectors might take a similar view to that of their Welsh counterparts.

My only reservation was that I did not wish to disappoint my father who always regarded himself as a fervent Welshman.

He accepted and respected my decision without any further discussion and continued to support me.

But I know it was a great thrill for him when some years later my brother John was selected to play rugby league for Wales.

England Come Calling

4

It was an agonising few days waiting for the English selectors' decision.

In the meantime I was being pilloried in the Welsh press, even appearing in a cartoon depicted as a black sheep.

Phil Horrocks-Taylor and Ricky Bartlett seemed to be the most likely England candidates and I had little confidence that I would make the first trial, 'Whites' versus 'Colours' in early December.

It was my 21st birthday just before and I received the most wonderful present when I got the news that I had been selected to play at Birmingham in the whites side alongside Dicky Jeeps, who was already acknowledged for his fine performances in the England shirt.

The whites was supposed to be the senior side, however only six of the previous season's England team were named, which gave an opportunity for newcomers like me to stake their claim.

I was up against another first-timer, Mike Weston from Durham.

He was a completely different type of player, keeping the opposition on the back foot with his prodigious tactical kicks.

I resolved to play my normal game, working with my team mates as much as possible, reading the play and trying to take any running chances if and when they came.

Despite lots of huffing and puffing, it was a scrappy game, neither side gained much of an advantage and the influential media were not particularly impressed.

We just won and I thought I had a reasonable match, mainly due to the magnificent Jeeps who guided me through.

I anxiously waited to read the weekend's papers.

H.B. Toft in the *Observer* summed up my performance with the comment that he still had to decide whether I was, 'brilliant but modest or discreet but limited.'

The Whites became 'Probables' and Colours the 'Possibles' for the second trial in Taunton.

Some of regulars returned and there were eight changes to the senior side.

I was surprised to find myself in the Probables with Jeeps as Phil Horrocks-Taylor was now available but he was chosen opposite me.

The match was a non-event played in wind, rain and mud, horrible conditions, and finished without a point being scored.

I couldn't for the life of me see how it told the selectors anything but I survived and was chosen for England to play against 'The Rest' in the final trial at Twickenham on 3 January 1959, again paired with Jeeps.

Our opponents were Horrocks-Taylor and a new scrum-half from Cambridge University, Steve Smith, who had not played in any of the previous trials. He was one of the new breed; big, strong and with an amazing, long bullet-like pass, well ahead of his time and had been getting some rave reviews.

We had six new men in our ranks and the opposition contained seven internationals.

It was a cold but fine day, although the turf still boggy, for my first ever appearance at Twickenham and a great thrill even with only a few thousand in the ground.

The atmosphere was quite subdued, with the bulk shouting for the underdogs.

England won 13-9 and the general consensus was that hardly any players in the rest ranks had made a really strong bid for a place.

I thought I'd had my best game of the series, having scored a try with a couple of sidesteps and been given the goal kicking duties and landed two beauties.

I anxiously read the reports next day particularly Vivian Jenkins in the *Sunday Times* who had done a complete analysis of virtually every player on both sides.

He treated the half-backs as a pair and changed his mind at least three times about which set should be in, even anticipating what the ground conditions would be like a fortnight later at Cardiff Arms Park.

My head was in a whirl and when the news finally broke it was quite sensational, Steve Smith had been chosen and Jeeps, a candidate for captain, left out – but I was in.

I was ecstatic but also flabbergasted. Steve and I had never played together and hardly knew each other.

With him in the south and me based in Manchester, it meant that we would not meet until two days before the game.

Nowadays, everyone would be in camp for at least a

week and we would have had squad and bonding sessions beforehand.

There was no suggestion then that Steve and I might need to get together to understand each other's play – we were only playing for England after all!

The first match had to be against Wales what with all the controversy about my choice of country, my mettle was really going to be tested.

I had partnered long passers before like Leo Karseras and Frank Drewitt, but I had a preference for the quicker, shorter ball that I had received from such as Terry Humphries, Eddie Deasey and, of course, Dickie Jeeps.

Longer ones had the advantage of taking you well away from a rampaging wing-forward but the initial positioning of your run was critical as the ball was in the air longer.

With the short, quick pass there was more decision-making time with the ball in your hands, to weigh up the opposition and react accordingly.

Today, the talk is all about getting over the gain line against 'in your face' defences, the fly-half has very little thinking time.

Lying deeper would provide more options and uncertainty and reduce all the safety-first, aimless kicking that has prevailed in rugby union in recent times.

In the lead up to my first cap, I was on vacation from university and had the opportunity to spend some time at home with my family, reading the warm messages and telegrams of congratulations and good wishes for my debut on 15 January 1959.

Full of excitement and anticipation, I arrived at the hotel in Cardiff where the England team was ordered to assemble.

It was an opportunity for the debutants – Webb, Wackett, Bendon, Smith, Wightman and me – to meet seasoned internationals, the likes of Butterfield, Phillips, Thompson, Jackson, Marques and Higgins.

We certainly needed to listen to their words of wisdom.

Come the day, the weather conditions were perfect – for Wales. All the talk beforehand had been about the strength of their forwards against the attacking potential of the English backs.

Toft described it as: "The worst playing conditions since the Second World War – mud covered by straw to prevent the frost. Then came snow, then fog, then thaw and then a heavy relentless downpour falling continuously from early morning up to and throughout the game."

Despite that, the atmosphere at the famous Arms Park was electric.

We started our preparations unable to avoid hearing the sound of numerous, impromptu Welsh choirs giving vent to their passion in and around the ground.

As the pre-game tension rose in the changing room, the more experienced members went through their usual rituals.

Captain Butterfield was in total charge, there were no coaches in those days, and gave us our last minute instructions.

I have been party to hundreds of team talks but I can honestly say that apart from my habituated stretching programme of about ten minutes and, later in my career, a large mouthful of Oloroso sherry, I couldn't remember anything until I was on the field waiting for the kick-off.

My nerves were only calmed when I stood still for the national anthem and I must have been in some sort of trance from which I emerged just as the referee's whistle blew for the start of the game.

Suddenly we were in action and the Welsh tactics became immediately obvious.

They were going to take us on up front and pressurise the halves, concentrating on driving, kicking and mauling work close to the breakdown and keeping us on the back foot.

They even sacrificed possession at times and tried to force mistakes from us in the filthy weather.

Steve Smith and I had a torrid time and my first kick was charged down by the marauding Welsh back row of Clem Thomas, John Leleu and John Faull, ably supported by scrum half Lloyd Williams.

Steve was still throwing out his long passes but I was not always in the right place and some were going astray not least as the soaked ball was like a bar of soap.

The view afterwards was that we should have changed our tactics and, perhaps, taken the Welsh on at their own game but gradually we settled down, absorbed the pressure and there was still no score.

We started to gain some territory and my kicking game improved.

I tried a short chip and chase close to the Welsh line and hurled myself at the ball under a mass of Welsh bodies.

I'm certain to this day that I got the try but the referee, Irishman R.L. Williams, was not convinced I'd scored because he could not see the whitewash in the mud.

He disallowed it and that decision undoubtedly influenced the result.

There was nothing in it until late in the first half when Wales were close to our line and produced a moment of magic which proved to be decisive.

Debutant winger Dewi Bebb threw the ball into a line-out, hooker Bryn Meredith tapped it straight back to him and Bebb surprised our defence as he flew in at the corner without a hand being laid on him.

The Welsh had caught us napping and we'd given away a soft try. Terry Davies kicked a magnificent goal and Wales led 5-0.

Steve and I had now sorted out our teething troubles and started to get our superior back line moving, but the surface was now a bog and both teams were becoming unrecognisable, necessitating a clean set of jerseys at the break.

The second half was a stalemate as Wales continued to play it tight. I narrowly missed a difficult penalty kick from wide out as the ball dipped agonisingly under the crossbar and the Welsh defence prevailed, they had played the conditions better and deserved to hold on.

I could not get it out of my head that I had scored what could easily have been the winning try and was very surprised that, although it was mentioned in the reports, it was not seen as a big deal.

Imagine the scrutiny that would have gone on today with all the endless video replaying.

There was now a three week break before the next international against Ireland in Dublin on Valentine's Day.

There was no post mortem about what had happened in Wales, at least not among the players as everyone went their own way.

That was for the selectors to mull over as we went back to our club duties.

I played every Wednesday and Saturday in between and waited anxiously for their decision.

Thank goodness the all the new boys were to be given another chance at Lansdowne Road.

It was quite a different atmosphere in Dublin, less intimidating. The Irish were just as passionate but appeared to be full of bonhomie and charm at Lansdowne Road.

We had a last minute hiccough when Steve Smith went down with flu overnight and Dickie Jeeps was brought in at scrum-half.

I felt disappointed that we wouldn't have the opportunity to develop our partnership but I was quite happy to be playing with Dickie again as I felt he was my good luck charm, and he played a blinder.

The weather was good and the pitch perfect but the match overall was a great disappointment.

Ireland were all over us, playing in their typically ferocious high speed, trademark style, our forwards were overpowered but we defended well.

They seemed obsessed with getting the ball to their star man Tony O'Reilly in the centre and we harassed them into making errors as Malcolm Phillips did a good job on him.

In one brief moment in the opening forty minutes, we managed to get into their half and were awarded a penalty.

I was determined to take my chance this time and from a narrow angle the ball soared through the uprights for my first points for England and, totally against the run of play, gave us a 3-0 lead.

The Irish players and supporters were apoplectic and the match became more and more frenzied but with some luck and Irish mistakes – missed penalties and dropped balls – we held on and weathered the storm as they ran out of steam with twenty minutes to go and we recorded a famous victory.

The selectors largely kept faith for the next two matches but brought back Steve Smith for Dickie, despite his magnificent performance against Ireland.

On to a full Twickenham and the sacred turf for matches against France and Scotland.

They were memorable occasions but I have to say that the matches, which both finished 3-all, were bitterly disappointing both as a spectacle and from a playing point of view.

Jim Hetherington scored our penalty against France and we were rated the underdogs after their brilliant win against Scotland.

But, as on numerous other occasions, they had the Twickenham jitters and we should have won.

Against Scotland our forwards were second best again and the backs had limited chances but failed to deliver.

Once more hadn't scored a try again but I kicked a fifty-yard penalty.

Amazingly, with two draws, a win and only a narrow loss against Wales it could have been argued that we'd had a reasonable Championship, yet I was disillusioned about my first season in international rugby union.

England had not played well and I was an integral part of those poor performances.

Representing my country had been a wonderful honour and I'd enjoyed every occasion but I was dispirited about the quality of the rugby.

Despite some exciting moments, there was an element of safety first and an over concentration on defence in everything we did.

The laws as they stood favoured such play.

For example, the line out was a shambles with every man for himself as the ball was lobbed in by the wingers, giving both teams an almost equal chance of possession.

Referees awarded relatively few penalties and offences often went unpunished.

There was hardly any opportunity to express yourself freely with ball in hand which was my natural game.

It was an unwritten rule in internationals never to take the risk of passing the ball in your own half.

Although the weather had influenced the tactics in Wales, all the other matches had been played in near-perfect conditions.

But I was still ordered to kick on most occasions and gain ground up the touchline until we were in an attacking position in our opponents' half.

I smile to myself now when I tell people that on one occasion in the first half against Ireland, I thought I saw an opportunity to move the ball inside our own half instead of kicking, when the home defence for once was disorganised.

I passed the ball quickly to Jeff Butterfield who hurriedly kicked it into touch.

The air was blue as he remonstrated with me.

"I was only trying to play my normal game, Jeff,' I told him, receiving the reply: "Well don't play your xxxxx game here!"

There was lots of talk about sterile play and poor reward for the thousands of spectators, only eight tries had been scored in ten Five Nations matches and nine penalty goals.

Something needed to be done. The answer, as ever, was to change the laws.

We Ran with the Ball

5

The pinnacle of every British rugby union player's career is selection for the British Lions and the next tour, to Australasia, was looming in the summer of 1959.

Five Nations matches provided the opportunity to showcase credentials and the Lions selectors, two from each country, met a day after the England against Scotland game to make their final choice of the thirty men who would go on the four-and-a-half month trip of a lifetime.

Alf Wilson from Scotland had already been appointed manager and the press had all been promoting their favourites and making their predictions but there would be no announcement until all players chosen had been informed by letter.

I tried to keep calm as I weighed up my chances.

My rivals for the fly-half position were Cliff Ashton and Ken Richards from Wales, Ireland's Mick English, Gordon Waddell from Scotland possibly Phil Horrocks-

Taylor and Mike Weston who I had kept out of the England side. Cliff was, like me, in his first international season, Mick the most experienced, and Gordon had already captained Scotland.

I didn't know that Gordon was not available for the start of the tour because of examination commitments at Cambridge, Mick was duly recognised and I was overjoyed to be selected ahead of Cliff.

When I received the letter from Alf Wilson I got a real shock initially because it was addressed "Dear Gus"!

I was thrilled and only learned when the tour party was revealed to the press that Gordon had also been selected and would join the tour after his exams. He would be the utility back although my understanding was that he had hardly played in any other position than fly-half.

There were six weeks or so before the Lions were due to gather at Eastbourne on 16 May and players were advised that they should not play any rugby after 5 April.

We were expected to wrap ourselves in cotton wool, have a good rest after a long season and also avoid the risk of injury.

I had been almost completely injury free for nearly two seasons and played close on ninety matches in that time, so there was a temptation to put my boots away for a while.

The problem was I had just been invited to join the Barbarians annual Easter tour of South Wales for the first time which was an honour that every player craved, involving the best of the British Isles and normally a couple of top-line guests.

It was also an opportunity for an outstanding, long-serving club or county player who had, perhaps, just failed to achieve the highest honours to experience the top level.

The 'Babas' were world renowned for their

adventurous style of play with high risk passing from almost any part of the field, a dangerous strategy that was massively entertaining and enjoyable for players and spectators alike and, more often than not, very successful.

There was no way I could give up the chance, I was feeling great physically and mentally and really looking forward to what was certain to be an unforgettable get-together.

Several other Lions had been invited including Syd Millar, Ken Scotland, Ronnie Dawson – the Lions' captain – and Roddy Evans.

Playing alongside and mixing socially with them would be a helpful preparation for the tour if nothing else.

The matches were against Penarth, Cardiff, Swansea and Newport over the Easter weekend and I played in the opener, which was rather a drab affair as it turned out, and against Swansea which we won 18-11.

I had a bit of a wake-up call in that match because although I kicked four goals, the Welsh press commented on, 'a lack of pace' and, 'a slowness off the mark' and according to them I was apparently 'overshadowed' by the Swansea fly-half Brian Richards.

At the time I thought they were probably having a go at me because I was a 'deserter' but I resolved privately to keep their points in mind prior to the Lions tour.

One scary moment occurred when I came out of a tackle semi-concussed and bleeding and had to be carted off.

As was typical in those days of no replacements, I was summarily checked out on the touchline, bandaged up and thrown back on.

Fortunately for me it was nothing serious but for Peter Robbins, arguably England's best flanker, it was bad luck all the way.

After being dropped from the England team which many could not understand, he was then chosen for the Lions but broke his leg in the last match of the Babas tour and had to be replaced.

The prospect of being away for four-and-a-half months seemed daunting, but I was raring to go.

I was soon made aware of the complexity of such an operation when I started receiving masses of documents containing vital information with all the dos and don'ts from ultra-efficient secretary of the Four Home Unions tours committee, Peter Bradforth.

There was a great deal of material to absorb and every player was given a set of detailed instructions which had to be followed to the letter otherwise you would not be allowed on the plane.

The schedule was an organiser's nightmare, six matches in Australia, twenty-five in New Zealand and a couple in Canada on a route calling at Zurich, Beirut, Karachi, Calcutta, Singapore, Darwin and Melbourne in transit. Just getting my luggage together was difficult enough.

Advice was given on what to take in your 66lb baggage allowance; playing and training kit, footwear, official dress - formal and informal (number one and number two rig) raincoat, overcoat, drip dry shirts, camera, even jock straps – what to carry on the plane and what to go in the hold.

There were financial matters to take care of, what was paid for and what was not – travel expenses to Eastbourne were covered and we were to receive the princely sum of £3-10s per week allowance plus £2-10s vouchers for in-flight refreshments.

The bank manager had to be consulted on what other monies could or could not be carried as there were all sorts of restrictions.

I had to see the doctor and dentist for check-ups, have vaccinations for small pox and cholera, deal with insurance, sign agreements, order my kit, boots, official dress and, most important, make sure my passport was in order.

Mum and Dad were a great help.

I thought that my packing requirements were complicated but Dad reminded me of his third tour of Australia and New Zealand with the rugby league Lions during a time of rationing.

That was in 1946, and the party travelled to Australia on an aircraft carrier, *HMS Indomitable* which took six weeks to get there.

There was one other important issue to be dealt with, I was due to complete my final geology exams in June.

There were no special concessions in those days and the only solution suggested to me was to repeat my final year.

Although I was already almost through it, that seemed a perfect solution to me, a Lions tour and then another year as a student especially when my Local Education Authority in Cumberland very kindly agreed to continue my grant.

So I joined the rest of the British Lions tour party in Eastbourne and Jeff Butterfield's 'boot camp'.

Ronnie Dawson was already doubling up as captain and our only coach and Jeff was chosen as the one to try to whip us into shape in the four or five days we had together before boarding the plane to Australia.

Jeff's experience of the 1955 tour and his knowledge as a teacher of P.E. and sport seemed to provide him with the right credentials.

It was horrific! We were subjected to a fitness regime that would, from the very first day, have raised the eyebrows of the Marines.

We were hammered morning, noon and night.

It was a miracle that most of us managed to get through the agonies, stiffness and soreness and that included me, a self-professed keen trainer.

It was a crash course but we came through it and ready for a great adventure.

After a marathon journey and jet-lagged from three days of travel through all the time zones, we stood in the middle of the Olympic Stadium in Melbourne, where the Games had been held in 1948 and where we were due to play our first match against Victoria.

Friendships were already forming, Alan 'Neddy' Ashcroft was unanimously elected as our choirmaster, soon establishing a wide-ranging repertoire which was to become respected throughout Australia and New Zealand.

Tony O'Reilly was in charge of entertainment to be eventually joined by his mate Andy Mulligan and Gordon Wood was made judge and jury to deal with any acts of indiscipline or stupidity.

More characters emerged as the tour progressed and I linked up mainly with other younger members of the party in Malcolm Price, Ken Scotland and David Hewitt.

Rules were laid down and the tour philosophy on and off the field was made clear, very quickly establishing an air of togetherness prior to the first match.

Alf Wilson emphasised that our playing strategies would be built around pace and handling and that we would attempt to play attractive rugby at all times.

As a result of this we eventually became known as the, 'they ran with the ball' Lions.

Ronnie Dawson introduced his watchword P.A.C.E, standing for possession, attack, counterattack and endeavour.

Melbourne was steeped in Australian rules and

cricket with massive attendances but Victoria had virtually no rugby union tradition and the locals little genuine interest.

It was rather surreal as we ran on the field in the massive Olympic arena with only a few thousand spectators present but we were all well psyched up and raring to go wearing the Lions jersey for the first time.

We posted twelve tries in an overwhelming 53-18 performance and it was great to be selected for the opening match and I had a successful debut scoring two tries and six goals.

Immediately there were comparisons with my father who had become a legend in Australia on three tours.

He was a hard act to follow and my links with rugby league through him were to become a matter of great controversy.

The Australian press were full of praise and admiration for our performance, John Young our Olympic sprinter had astonished everyone with his electrifying pace as did Peter Jackson – nicknamed Nicholai for some reason – on the other wing with his elusiveness.

But we, and especially me, got a shock when we got to Sydney for our next match against New South Wales.

It appeared that I was the centre of raging controversy in the press.

The New South Wales Rugby League had invited me to attend a luncheon in honour of my father's supreme exploits in Australia which was brought to the attention of Alf Wilson and I was refused permission to go.

I was bitterly disappointed although he explained to me and the press that no individual could accept any private invitation.

The press were determined to make a big issue of the decision raising the union against league and professional versus amateur debate, and trying to create trouble in the British camp prior to the match against the state side.

I felt it had been an honest invitation and it was a real snub to them when Alf seemed determined to keep to the letter of the law.

I must admit that I had not read the small print in our documentation and personally thought it was no big deal to allow me to go and represent the family.

My father had thousands of friends and admirers in this league-mad country and it was a great opportunity for them to pay their respects.

The decision was a disaster for our public relations at the time but I was still able to meet informally with many of Dad's friends who contacted me by letter, telephone, simply turning up at the hotel or meeting in the street.

From then on, throughout the tour, my own nickname became Bev 'friends of my dad' Risman.

We were treated to wonderful hospitality from our hosts with receptions leading up to the match and banquets, where I developed a taste for king prawns, and our first introduction to the poker machines, on which many of us made contributions to the local economy.

The alcohol flowed freely and everyone took full advantage.

I was one of only four to retain their place for the NSW clash and, despite the squad being hailed in the build-up by none other than J.G.B. Thomas as having 'the stamp of greatness', we came a real cropper as they stopped our attempts to run the ball freely and pulled off a well merited 18-14 victory.

Their half-backs Arthur Summons and 19-year-old future international Ken Catchpole controlled the game, Arthur teaching me another valuable lesson.

We were not helped by the first of many serious injuries which were to hamper us throughout the tour when Niall Brophy lasted only three minutes, suffering an ankle injury which turned out to be so serious that his participation ended there and then.

Nevertheless, with only fourteen men we were still leading with ten minutes to go but just could not last out.

The press thought that I had played, 'a steady game' but I wasn't happy with my performance having been kept pretty much shackled throughout.

After only two fixtures, uncertainty seemed to be arising about the goal-kicking situation because we were well aware that if we had landed our goals, we would have won.

That problem was to haunt us later in the tour.

We had six recognised goal kickers in the party; Terry Davies, David Hewitt, Ken Scotland, John Faull, Malcolm Thomas and me.

Terry was regarded as the number one, way ahead of the rest of us, but we all took our turn. I'd always kicked goals from early schooldays and was quite happy to be given the duty and responsibility.

Unfortunately, I don't remember it being mentioned in our team talks or any of us spending hours on the training ground practising the art.

There didn't seem to be a pecking order throughout the tour and I was never really sure who would be given the duties for a particular match which was to cost us as it turned out, we ended up only converting about half of the tries we scored overall.

We had to put the defeat behind us and immediately focus on the next matches against Queensland followed by the First Test in Brisbane only four days later.

We overran the state side playing outstanding

running rugby to get us back on track and everyone waited anxiously for the Test line-up to be announced.

Australia had already selected their side of whom all but two had beaten us the previous week.

Mick English played fly-half for us against Queensland, his first match of the tour and I still regarded him as first choice.

I'm not sure whether Mick was fully fit and injury was to haunt him too and I got the nod as the names; Scotland, Jackson, Price, Hewitt, O'Reilly, Risman, Jeeps, Faull, Smith, Williams, Mulcahy, Ashcroft, Miller, Dawson and McLeod were read out.

It was an incredibly proud moment.

The game was played in 40-degree heat on a rock hard surface at the Exhibition Ground Brisbane, conditions which were totally alien to us.

We surprised the Aussies by playing a much more controlled game than they had anticipated, conserving our energies in the heat and looking for territory, and coming on strongly in the second half to run out comfortable winners 17-6.

After the heat and hard grounds of the previous two matches, several players were suffering from severe grass burns and a revolutionary precaution was proposed for the next match – to wear women's nylons.

There was understandable media interest in the build-up to the Second Test heightened by the propaganda war between league and union when it was announced that the simultaneous 13-a-side Test, between the Green and Golds and Kiwis, would have an earlier kick off so there would be an opportunity for spectators to watch some part of both games which, apparently, a fair number did.

The Wallabies had already announced an unchanged

Early years: Aged nine, with Mum Ethel and Dad Gus, carrying brother John.
Dad, in army uniform, *inset*, is about to move to Workington as player-coach.
Below: On the stand at a Salford 'Red Devils' rugby league match with my first
half-time orange. Dad will soon be called up for War service in the Army.

School days – winter: Cockermouth Grammar school, 1952-53. Captaining my first rugby union team from scrum-half. A happy band! I also played for Cumberland Under 15s. We won most of our matches.

School days – summer: Cockermouth GS first XI, 1955. George Griffiths, our PE master, is beside me and gave important advice on how to manage my future. Frank Foster, third left back row, also later played professional rugby league.

Up the rankings: Captaining the 1956 England RU Schools U18s against Wales at Gloucester. John Young, front third left, became a GB Olympic sprinter and fellow British Lion. Mike Wade, fourth right back, would also go on to play for England.

College days: Playing fly-half for Loughborough 1960/1961, while studying for my Post Grad teaching diploma, extreme left front row. I seem to end up sitting or kneeling on the grass a lot at this stage!

Pride of Lancashire: Eric Evans was our distinguished captain. Alan Ashcroft of England and the British Lions is middle row third left. Reg Higgins, second right, and John Wilcox, back row extreme right, also played for England. Dave Parker, centre back row, was my captain at Manchester University and went on to play for Oldham and Great Britain in rugby league. I am seated front row left.

Above: England v Wales, Cardiff, 1959, during my third year at Manchester University.

Left: Wearing the North West Counties jersey. I also played against Australia in 1958.

Souvenir pennant: The Rismans at home, circa 1959.

Father and sons: Taken when I got my England Under 18 Schools rugby union shirt. Dad wears his Great Britain rugby league shirt. Brother John is too young to have his international shirt, but will play rugby league for Wales.

Below: Ready to go on tour.

Cartoon:
Caricature of me in the New Zealand press

"The fly-half was a beautiful player to watch. He had a flashing sidestep off either foot, his punts were accurate and he was a competent goal kicker. His hands impressed many – he could catch a ball it seemed from all and every position and circumstance. But it was also his tackling, especially cover tackling when the situation looked hopeless, that lifted him out as a special character."

Legends of World Rugby, Paul Verdon

A.B.W. RISMAN
GEOLOGY STUDENT
FAST. ASTUTE TACTICAL KICKER.

British Lions 1959: Australia and New Zealand Tour. Row by row from back (*left to right*): David Hewitt (Ireland), Malcolm Price (Wales), Peter Jackson (England), Andy Mulligan (Ireland), Haydon Morgan (Wales), Gordon Wood (Ireland); Syd Millar (Ireland), Ray Prosser (Wales), Niall Brophy (Ireland), Ken Smith (Scotland), Alan Ashcroft (England), Gordon Waddell (Scotland), Terry Davies (Wales); Bill Mulcahy (Ireland), John Faull (Wales), Roddy Evans (Wales), David Marques (England), Rhys Williams (Wales), Tony O'Reilly (Ireland), Stan Coughtrie (Scotland), Noel Murphy (Ireland); Hughie Macleod (Scotland), Malcolm Thomas (Wales), Alf Wilson (manager), Ronnie Dawson (capt, Ireland), Ossie Glasgow (treasurer), Jeff Butterfield (England), Bryn Meredith (Wales); Dickie Jeeps (England), John Young (England), Ken Scotland (Scotland), Bev Risman (England), Mick English (Ireland).

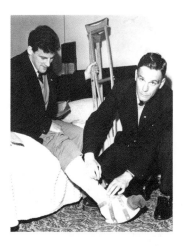

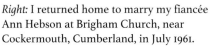

Highs and lows: Bad luck, *left,* in New Zealand in 1959 when I miss the second and third Tests with a broken ankle. Peter Jackson (nicknamed Nikolai) signs my plaster cast.

Right: I returned home to marry my fiancée Ann Hebson at Brigham Church, near Cockermouth, Cumberland, in July 1961.

On the beach: The Lions relax on a pre-tour get together in Eastbourne.
Neddie Ashcroft has his guitar, captain Ronnie Dawson looks on from the
deckchair ... and that's me posing in the dark glasses and Speedos!

More Lions leisure-time: Here I am on the left while Ken Scotland, my best mate
on tour, is at the front. We are still good friends and he still beats me at golf.

side while we were struggling to find 15 men thanks to an ever horrendous injury list. Fortunately, all our form backs were declared fit but the weather was filthy as the rain poured down and the Sydney Sports Ground became awash so we never did get to wear those tights.

We led narrowly and, just before half-time, the weather abated and as the pitch quickly dried out, we treated the spectators to an exhibition of spectacular handling, running rugby, scoring four more tries to run out convincing 24-3 winners to clinch the series.

I was beginning to feel quite at home on the tour and was delighted to be part of a team that had done so well, especially as I scored a significant try early in the second half, which received considerable mention in the press.

I had seen a disorganised defence in front of me and decided to have a go at them, successfully putting into practice all the evasive skills I had learned in the school yard years before.

Paul Vardon in his book *Kings of Rugby* describes it as, 'One of the finest individual tries the tourists would score.' I don't know about that but I certainly enjoyed the moment.

We were battered and bruised when we left Australia twenty hours after the Second Test, with a worrying crop of wounded, some quite serious.

However, after six weeks together, we had blended into a close-knit, harmonious group and spirits were high as we were met by the New Zealand officials.

After a lavish reception and overnight stay in Auckland, we immediately flew to Napier, a beautiful coastal holiday city on North Island for our match with Hawkes Bay.

We were met by a huge crowd at the airport and the cheering and waving continued as our cavalcade wound its way through the streets to the city.

It felt as if we were royalty and we began to realise how much of a rugby-obsessed nation this was. The vast majority study the game, its history and culture.

When I returned with Ann for a private holiday fifty years later, I was accosted by a senior customs official who looked at my name in the passport and instantly remembered me playing in the First Test in Dunedin and all the incidents that occurred, while at the same time fining me 200 dollars for accidentally bringing an illegal orange into the country!

Our performances in Australia had been impressive and the NZ press had given us a big build up but we knew that the real examination was still to come.

I wasn't one of those who professed to never reading the newspaper reports and articles and I become totally absorbed in page after page of the coverage that appeared every day.

You could not fail to be impressed by the comprehensive analysis of individuals and tactics by New Zealand journalists like Eric Boggs, Bill Boshier and Terry McLean and the famed Winston McCarthy on the radio.

We had brought our own experts in Vivian Jenkins and J.B.G. Thomas and I studied their reports with interest, comparing their version of events to those of the local media.

As we settled in at Napier, we were at last able to take a few deep breaths as we had a full week to prepare for the match against Hawkes Bay, weigh up the magnitude of this latest adventure and take stock of our progress so far.

We were about to embark on a whistle-stop programme of activities throughout a beautiful country and its exquisite scenery and begin to appreciate the fascinating Maori culture.

I was very disappointed not to be selected for the opening fixture.

Gordon Waddell, fresh from arriving, was thrown in at the deep end and Mick English and I were left to kick our heels.

I was really buzzing after Australia and felt at peak fitness, I'd established myself as the number one fly-half and thought we should have selected the strongest possible team first up to set down a marker for the rest of the tour.

After the six matches in Australia, and even allowing for competition for places, some sort of pecking order had been established but, as it turned out, the mounting injury toll dictated selection considerably.

Hawkes Bay has a great tradition of victories against touring teams and although they were not at this time one of the strongest provinces, there was a feeling among the 21,000 strong crowd, on a glorious afternoon, that the Lions were there for the taking.

They scored first but from that moment we totally dominated, the backs ran riot as we posted 13 touchdowns, David Hewitt claiming four and Ken Scotland a hat-trick.

Our 52-12 win was the highest scored against a provincial side, we had made a statement and shocked a nation.

The press had a field day. Vivian Jenkins described the victory as: "The most exciting rugby experience ... no tidal wave could have made a bigger impact."

Terry McLean noted: "A golden haze descended on the Lions Tour at the opening match."

Great praise indeed as we basked in the glory, remembering that it was the New Zealand press who had originally criticised our rigorous training sessions as being 'lackadaisical'.

I was upset to have not been part of the jamboree and missed out again against Poverty Bay, East Coast at Gisborne,

Mick English was selected at fly-half and Gordon Waddell in the centre.

I was totally fed up, seven players had to double up due to our injury crisis and I believed that I was the only player who was fit but had not been chosen.

There was no explanation given, I was raring to go but was left on the side lines again.

Still, I had to bite the bullet, and there were no assurances that I would be selected for the next match, a big one against Auckland.

Fortunately, I was recalled and we won 15-10 in front of 60,000 spectators, many queuing overnight for a match remembered mainly for the hosts, 'spirited and aggressive' resistance and a major incident of foul play.

In teaching us the essence of ruck play, according to Vivian Jenkins, Albie Prior, the Auckland flanker, 'Danced upon Marques' head' in what was clearly a sending- off offence, but apparently not according to the referee.

No action was taken afterwards and Prior kept his place for the next match which soured the off-field relationships.

We girded our loins accordingly and prepared to go blow-for-blow but fortunately left North Island for the next leg of the tour and the controversy died down. We flew to Christchurch and into what seemed another world.

The build up to the First Test against the All Blacks in Dunedin was starting but we had only eighteen fit players for the game against NZ Universities and I found myself suddenly appearing in my second match in four days as the only fit fly-half.

Fortunately the students couldn't live with our expansive play and the game was effectively won by half-time

We relaxed, the Universities rallied and set up an exciting finale for the 45,000 fans but we won 25-3 in the end. Late in the game I picked up a knee injury which caused concern about my availability for the Test, due in less than three weeks' time.

Apart from the occasional bump and bruise, I had been injury free for a couple of years.

It was one of those where you can't tell how serious the damage is for the first few days because of the swelling.

I'd bent it backwards and stretched the tendons but couldn't ascertain whether there had been any cartilage or ligament damage, and there were no immediate scans in those days.

I began to panic that I'd miss out on playing against the All Blacks, the world's best.

The injury lists got longer, our resources more threadbare and we crashed against Otago and lost our precious unbeaten record in New Zealand.

We had no expert medical staff with us and had to rely on cover by New Zealand doctors and physios for our diagnosis and treatment.

It didn't seem as though much was being done for me, rest and gentle exercise was the prescription but that only caused more frustration as I jogged about but couldn't feel discernible progress.

I was still favouring the leg in the week leading up to the opening encounter and there was added pressure because Mick English had been ruled out of the rest of the tour with a serious injury and was on his way home.

Gordon Waddell was unfit and there was even talk of Ken Scotland filling in at fly-half but then full-back Terry Davies, who had been playing well, withdrew and Ken was earmarked to play there.

Both Sides of the Fence

I was picked regardless of my injury which was making slow but steady progress.

I knew I wasn't fully fit and it was a terrible dilemma because I'd not had any opportunity to evaluate the knee under match conditions.

I'd not played for three weeks but was now running at almost full speed although there was still some discomfort.

It was ultimately my decision and I opted to take the risk and declare myself fit.

I survived the match and took part in, arguably, the most controversial Test of all time.

The Battle of Dunedin

6

All of New Zealand seemed to have converged on Dunedin for the First Test. The Carisbrooke ground had a capacity of 41,500 but thousands were unable to get in and tried to get vantage points all around the bowl.

There was the 'Scotsman's grandstand' which provided free viewing from the railway embankment and dozens of temporary structures erected in gardens with views of the pitch.

Health and safety took a back seat and apparently 276 casualties were dealt with as kick off drew near. Only Cardiff Arms Park could provide anything like the atmosphere.

What unfolded that afternoon was arguably the greatest travesty of justice that ever occurred on a rugby field, in my opinion.

The result, 18-17 to the All Blacks, was not so remarkable, but the way the win was achieved was truly unbelievable.

The New Zealand total was made up of six penalty goals kicked by Don Clarke. The Lions scored four tries of which only one was converted.

The result hinged almost entirely on the decisions of home referee Alan Fleury.

The enormity of it did not really strike home until late in the game because the Lions were completely in control for 65 minutes.

We were leading 17-9 and were still ahead by two points with just a few minutes to go.

We had totally outplayed the All Blacks with our exciting brand of expansive rugby, Malcolm Price with two, Tony O'Reilly and Peter Jackson were our try scorers as we ran rampant.

Little significance was attached to our missed goal kicks until the final whistle while Don Clarke was the home hero, capable of potting goals from immense distances, he proved to be the difference.

It was only when we got back to the changing room that the shock hit us.

Controversy raged in the press for days afterwards.

The statistics showed that Mr. Fleury awarded thirty-five penalties in all, twenty-one to the All Blacks and fourteen for us but, significantly, four were awarded to the hosts in the last ten minutes and all but one within range of the posts.

The other was on the New Zealand line when the Lions were in a try scoring position.

Although referees are frequently much maligned, there can be no denying the influence that those decisions had on the outcome.

One All Blacks penalty kick at goal had even been waved away by Mick English, our touch judge, but his decision was overruled by Mr. Fleury.

The New Zealand and British press revelled in the controversy but most agreed that what had happened should not have.

There is no doubt that this encounter was quoted on many occasions when discussions on changes to the scoring system eventually led to the five point try. In virtually all departments except goal kicking, it was recognised that we'd had the measure of the mighty All Blacks.

There was some panic in the New Zealand ranks as thoughts turned to the rest of the Tour, which had really only just begun.

Our backline of Scotland, Hewitt, Price and Jackson had run amok and our forwards had more than held their own, giving Dick Jeeps and me the opportunity to control the game. I felt that I had played well enough and was greatly relieved that my knee had stood the strain of a full eighty minutes.

We had seven provincial matches to play before the Second Test and I had a really good run, appearing in four of them. We won six and lost narrowly against Canterbury with only thirteen men as injuries continued to bite and play havoc with selection.

I found myself selected to play in two midweek matches as the only fir fly-half with Gordon Waddell chosen at full-back.

Against Wanganui, I received quite a buffeting from the opposition who obviously targeted me and the referee, Mr. S.G. Lennon allowed them to break every rule in the book. One of his decisions, in which I was involved, has gone down in history as one of the most bizarre incidents ever seen in a rugby match.

We received a rare penalty award about 45 yards from goal and as I was about to take the kick, ball placed and run up all set, a police officer marched on to the pitch and tapped the referee on the shoulder.

The entire crowd screamed at the referee as the constable drew the official's attention to a Wanganui touch judge standing erect with his flag up, apparently for some time. Referee Lennon brushed the policeman aside, told him to leave the pitch and me to continue with the penalty kick.

The kick was successful, the referee awarded the goal and then decided to consult with his touch judge, promptly cancelled the score and called a line-out.

It could have made all the difference to the result but we squeezed home, 9-6.

I was left out of the big weekend match against Taranaki but was required to play in a game at Palmerston North against the combined side Manawatu Horohenowa just four days before the Second Test.

It was a great contest because they decided to play us at our own game which provided some spectacular entertainment.

The pitch was very firm and half way through the second half we were leading quite convincingly when I went over on my ankle.

I carried on for a while but it was niggling me and it was decided that I should come off as a precaution.

It turned out to be worse than was thought so I went to hospital and the next thing I knew the leg was in plaster up to the knee, I was told it was broken just above the ankle.

My first thought was that I would be out of the Second Test in Wellington and then it dawned on me that my tour could be over – I was understandably devastated and, for a while, inconsolable.

There was no second opinion and it was even suggested in the press that there may have been some medical subterfuge, had someone been too hasty with the plaster?

I did make a remarkable recovery and I was grateful to the management who decided that I could stay on for the rest of the tour and, as it turned out, less than five weeks later I was fit to play in the last three matches.

Wellington was engulfed with people determined to be at the Second Test, thousands were locked out and gates pulled down as fans climbed over barbed wire fences, with no consideration for health and safety.

There were multiple changes in both teams, the Lions had sent for Bill Patterson but did not have a single fly-half fit to play.

Desperate measures were needed and Malcolm Price who had not played in the role since his schooldays was moved from centre and thrown in at the deep end.

The All Blacks also made tactical changes.

It was another titanic struggle and, despite their weakened team, the Lions out played the All Blacks and fully deserved to win.

It looked on the cards until, with us leading 8-6 and only a couple of minutes to go, Don Clarke again denied us our just desserts, this time with a try and we lost 11-8.

The next few weeks were just a blur for me as I tried to come to terms with my injury and remain positive.

I was told that the plaster should remain on for three weeks at least and then there would be a reassessment and, in the interim, I was wandering around on crutches trying to make light of the travel and keep up with the tour party.

We had three matches to play in the build up to the Third Test in Christchurch, during which time I had to get used to keeping myself occupied.

There were occasions when I really thought that it

would be better for everyone if I packed up and went home but I clung to the thought that I could possibly recover in time for the Fourth Test and tried to stay involved as much as possible.

We were now in real farming country in South Island and spent much time in local communities who feted us wherever we went.

We won all three provincial matches including the one in King Country when we came up against the legendary Colin 'pine tree' Meads, the All Blacks hard man lock forward.

Colin and his mates attempted to soften us up and the match turned ugly as Tony O'Reilly, of the playboy looks, came in for special treatment.

The King's were getting increasingly exasperated but on this occasion we were fortunate to have a referee, Mr Robson, who was having none of it and kept the penalties for foul play totting up.

Throughout the tour, the rough house tactics of the provincial teams was a popular strategy to intimidate us and referees tended to turn a blind eye even penalising the Lions for 'over-aggressive retaliation.'

Even Don Clarke, playing for Waikato where he was a cult hero, was far from blameless.

He had a nightmare when we played there, missing all his goals and was responsible for a couple of unsavoury incidents – the god was human after all.

Honesty compels me to admit that, of course, we had tough guys in our ranks, it's safe to say that Ray Prosser, Rhys Williams, Syd Millar and Bill Mulcahy were no angels.

The build up to the Third Test was electric, we had a last chance to keep the series alive although being agonisingly unfit I struggled to feel part of it.

However, Christchurch proved to be a huge anti-climax, the impressive All Blacks put a convincing performance and stuffed us 22-8, with Don Clarke again at his imperious best.

The defeat affected us badly, we had been away from home for nearly four months, lost three games in the four match Test series and had to get up at the crack of dawn to travel to Wellington.

It was a subdued and downcast bunch that staggered on to the plane for the next leg.

We had been a very harmonious group but spirit would really be tested as there were five more matches to be played and we had to pull ourselves round.

Tony O'Reilly and Andy Mulligan sensed the despondency and decided to do something about it.

They had been a source of great amusement throughout the tour with their excellent leadership and humour and, on this occasion, persuaded the cabin crew to let them use the microphone on the plane.

The pair proceeded to entertain everyone on board with a hilarious hour of comedy including jokes, stories and impersonations of various members of the party, recalling the best moments, including the 'friends of my dad' story.

I had just had the plaster cast removed and was determined to get fit to play again.

We had nothing to be ashamed about, had received accolades for our style of play and now that the pressure was off, could approach the rest of the tour in a more relaxed manner and target a win in the final Test.

The All Blacks wanted a clean sweep and we were equally determined to be only the second side to win a last Test.

I worked frantically in training but secretly still had a

lot of pain and stiffness in the ankle and kept it strapped up for all the sessions.

I watched us play the Maoris and had to endure yet another match where the opposition tried to batter us into submission and what could have been an outstanding encounter deteriorated into a series of punch ups.

Our toughies, Roddy Evans, Bill Mulcahy and Noel Murphy cheerfully handed out the retribution and those of us on the side lines watched with sly amusement as Ray Prosser acted as peacemaker.

The last match before the Fourth Test was against North Auckland and it was make or break for me if I was to have any chance of selection for the Test team.

I was given the opportunity to prove my fitness and have never been so nervous before a game.

Worse, I slipped on the stairs on the morning of the game and broke into a cold sweat as I felt a sharp pain in the ankle.

For a minute or two I felt that my comeback attempt was all over but gradually the ache eased and I said nothing.

I don't know whether it was designed to help me forget the injury but I was made captain for the day and one of my most treasured memories is leading the British Lions out.

It was decided that we should field the strongest side available in preparation for the final showdown and although North Auckland tried to physically intimidate us early on, their tactics were put in the shade by a thundering display from our forwards and we won convincingly.

For me, it was a matter of survival, I was targeted early on and received a very dubious belt on the nose after the ball had gone which drew blood and stirred me up and I completed the match with no further ill effects.

We spent a weekend touring the idyllic Bay of Islands before we got down to the business of our final challenge.

All the media talk was of the All Blacks completing the whitewash but we were determined to finish the tour all guns blazing and, with the pressure off, were more relaxed.

We felt we'd played in the right manner throughout and entertained the spectators and that had been appreciated, witnessed by a 63,000 capacity crowd turning up at Eden Park.

More or less for the first time on tour, Dickie Jeeps apart, everyone was fit and available.

Ronnie Dawson, whose place had come under threat from experienced hooker Bryn Meredith, led us out and the crowd, squeezed into every corner of the famous stadium went wild, even though there'd been a deluge in the build-up. The weather had cleared but with two curtain raisers having been played on it, the pitch was a quagmire which didn't really suit our style.

We were forced into playing a much tighter game and my job was to keep our pack moving forward with tactical kicking and stretching Don Clarke at the back.

The plan was to create errors in the home defence and only run the ball when we had engineered space and it was working. We chose our moments and came up with two tries, a mesmerising run from Peter Jackson and a typically powerful charge by Tony O'Reilly for his record-breaking 17th touchdown on tour.

The New Zealand backs rarely threatened but our only failure was again goal kicking, we missed both conversions and two Clarke penalties had us level.

Then came the greatest moment in my rugby union career.

With five minutes to go, Andy Mulligan who had

been tormenting the New Zealand back row, set off on a cross field run from a scrum taking all their back row with him.

As he ran across in front of me, I slowed down to let him pass, I wasn't actually anticipating getting the ball but suddenly he flicked a reverse pass and it was in my hands.

I looked up to see a wall of defenders in front of me with no opening in sight, so I veered towards the blind side round the back of the scrum as it broke up.

All the defenders bar Bruce McPhail, their right winger, had disappeared and a way to the line opened up.

From that point everything seemed to be happening as if a slow motion film.

Bruce stood, isolated like a statue, blocking my way to the try line, I knew he was faster than me and I couldn't hope to run round him.

If ever there was a time to use my famed sidestep, this was it and I left him on the ground grasping at thin air.

Out of the corner of my eye, I saw three All Black cover defenders desperately closing in but I had a head start and accelerated into open space and sprinted the last thirty yards to the line, ending with a triumphant dive.

The histrionic celebrations now was just not done in those days and, despite my elation, photographs show that I look positively glum as Ronnie Dawson gently put his arm round me as he beckoned Terry Davies to take the conversion attempt.

There were fifteen minutes still to go but sections of the crowd began shouting 'red, red, red' for the Lions and it was an awesome feeling when the final whistle went and we had achieved a tremendous victory.

That was almost the end of a unique experience.

New Zealand and Australia had been wonderful hosts and we visited Fiji, Hawaii, San Francisco and Canada –

playing two pioneering matches in Vancouver and Toronto – before finally calling in for sightseeing in New York.

I gained a long-term golf partner too in Ken Scotland who very kindly noted as we returned to these shores: "On the pitch the tactics were very largely dependent on who was playing at fly-half.

"In all, because of injuries, seven players filled this crucial position. They all brought their own particular merits to it but the finest all-rounder and the one who brought out the best in the players roundabout him was Bev."

In 2009, we had a fifty-year reunion of the squad in Paris organised by Tony O'Reilly and his wife Chrissie, where skipper Ronnie Dawson summed up a momentous time in our lives.

"What a delight it was for those of us who could attend to have this opportunity to meet once again," he noted. "As with all such gatherings, the reminiscences and stories abounded and became more fanciful and exaggerated as the evening wore on.

"Without question the 1959 Lions Tour is remembered for the quality of our backs. This attacking play required correct control at outside half and was well orchestrated by Bev. From his international debut, he displayed his range of playing skills. He was a very balanced runner, had wonderful judgement, quick and decisive both in attack and defence with great finishing ability and was a good goal kicker."

He continued: "Rugby football is but one small part of what life has to offer, but what a pleasant part for those who participate.

"At the reunion we reflected on our good fortune to have had the benefit of such experiences and enjoyment, but comradeship and enduring friendships made are the abiding memories."

In the Wilderness

7

I had just completed the trip of a life time cramming into four-and-a-half months enough incidents, accidents, excitement, agony and delirium to last me for the rest of my rugby playing days.

I had to keep reminding myself I was still only 22.

On returning, I had hardly come back to earth and been re-introduced to the family before I was being thrown into the deep end of a new season.

Ann had kept me happy with numerous letters during the time apart but no sooner had we been reunited, then we had to leave each other again.

While I had been away, she'd graduated and was embarking on a post graduate course at Nottingham while I had to complete my final year in Manchester.

It meant regular weekend trips there after our Saturday matches and back again on late Sunday or early Monday morning for lectures.

As for rugby, I felt on top of the world, far from being jaded after no break from the game for two seasons, I was raring to go.

I'd just been chosen as one of the five outstanding players of the year by the prestigious New Zealand Almanac as a result of our performances in Australia and New Zealand, an honour which I could hardly have dreamt about at the start of the tour.

It was a reflection of the quality of Lions performances that four out of five players chosen were from the tourists and mind-boggling to think that, according to the New Zealand authorities, I was the best fly-half in the world.

It was to be a very short reign.

The highlight at the start of the 1959-60 season was a special match arranged in celebration of the golden jubilee of Twickenham.

A combined England and Wales team played against Scotland and Ireland with the sides made up of all the available Lions plus several other international guests.

It was a wonderful occasion, not just meeting up with all my mates from the tour again but because the game turned out to be a superb exhibition of all that was best in rugby union.

Running and passing in true Barbarian style, although the score was largely irrelevant, the match was highly competitive and it was good to be on the winning side with the result in doubt until the last few minutes.

It appeared from the press reports that I had become established on the international scene and I got stuck in to the annual programme of club and county matches in the build up to the interminable England trials.

As far as selection was concerned you still had to go through three of them regardless of your status.

I was favourite to retain my place ahead of old rivals Mike Weston and Phil Horrocks-Taylor with new boy Richard Sharp coming up on the rails, although Mike was then switched to centre.

My build up to the international season was perfect, I was playing two fixtures a week at university and in all the county clashes for Lancashire, and was duly selected for the international against Wales at Twickenham when I picked up a slight hamstring strain in training.

I was in a panic as to whether I would recover in time and was forced to inform the selectors about the problem.

I didn't think it was serious as I'd had slight strains like that before and was making good progress in the week before the match.

I turned up with the rest of the squad at our Richmond hotel as scheduled on the Thursday with a view to having a run out with the team as usual.

Just as a precaution, a reserve was sent for as no replacements were allowed during the match and Richard Sharp was called up, which was a surprise although he had been getting rave notices for Oxford University.

I felt under pressure to declare myself fit and was desperate to play and gave myself a thorough workout in the sprints and practices during our Friday afternoon training.

Ominously, I could feel some discomfort which gradually got worse as the session progressed.

It wouldn't have been fair to take a chance and then let everyone down in such an important game, I hated it but felt that it was right to withdraw.

My loss was Richard's gain. He turned up after a long trip from his home in Cornwall and only had time for a short practice with captain Dickie Jeeps.

Richard had a daunting task ahead of him and I had

to swallow my disappointment and try to help out with his brief preparation for by far the biggest day in his rugby life.

I thought back to my debut at the same time the previous year in Cardiff but I'd had several days to get mentally and physically ready.

He took everything in his stride and cut the Welsh to ribbons.

Richard and I were like chalk and cheese. I was dark, short and stocky, a ducker and diver who liked to take on defences with side steps and a variety of tactical kicks.

He was blonde, lanky and graceful, a master of the outside break and a prodigious kicker and drop goal expert.

England won and Richard was the star, I couldn't begrudge him his success but the worst was yet to come for me.

Having recovered from my hamstring problem, I was available for the next match against Ireland and waited expectantly for news of my selection.

It never came and I eventually learned that Richard had retained the fly-half spot and I had been dropped, I received no contact or explanation.

The decision took some stomaching, my international career had suddenly ground to a halt and there would be no opportunity to fight my way back into the team unless Richard played poorly or the selectors had another rush of blood.

As it turned out, he continued to play very well, England won the Triple Crown and shared the championship with France and I spent the rest of the season playing club and representative rugby at student level and in the occasional invitational team.

With final exams coming up in June, I had more time to get on with my neglected studies and although I was never the most enthusiastic academic, I finished with an honours degree in geology, one of my more satisfying achievements.

I had decided to apply for a post graduate diploma in physical education at Loughborough College with a view to becoming a PE teacher and started to look forward to yet another year as a student and a career in sport.

Loughborough had the reputation of being the top establishment in the country for PE and as well as obtaining a teaching qualification, there would be the opportunity to spend time training at the highest level alongside international sportsman in other sports, such as athletes John Sherwood and Alan Pascoe.

Inevitably, being left out of the England team meant that there was some talk about whether I would turn professional and my father had several enquiries about my intentions.

Deep down that was still my dream and it was tempting to consider the options yet I was still young and my plans were to complete my year at Loughborough and get my qualifications in place.

Anyway, I had some unfinished business in union, to try to win back my place in the England team.

Being at Loughborough with outstanding sports facilities and expert tuition, we were introduced to all the new training methods, including Graham Adamson's revolutionary circuit training, which meant we had every opportunity to reach and maintain peak fitness.

Having been on the Lions tour, I was regarded as something of a celebrity initially but was soon brought down to earth competing against and playing with many extremely dedicated and skilled, high class athletes from other sporting disciplines.

As we got to the 1960-61 rugby season, I was really

enjoying playing for the college team. We were all incredibly fit, much more so than most of the opposing student sides and other rugby clubs and we played an exciting brand of rugby, attempting to run the opposition off its feet.

My fitness was a great advantage when playing for Lancashire and everything seemed back on track as the time came round for the International trials.

I'd been playing well and was looking forward to the task of getting in the selectors minds again.

As the international season approached, there were some rumblings in the press about the fly-half options and even some talk about both Richard Sharp and myself being selected.

There was no question of Richard playing in an alternative position but speculation whether I could be moved to centre or full-back, with inevitable comparison to my father who'd operated so brilliantly in both roles.

My only real experience of playing at international level in either position was as a reserve for English Schools when I was drafted in at centre when Mike Wade withdrew just before the match against Wales.

There was no word about the situation from the selectors until the trials came round and lo-and-behold I found myself chosen at centre for the 'Possibles' in the second trial at Banbury, and for 'The Rest' in the final one at Twickenham.

To be honest, I could never see myself as a centre but I was happy to give it a go rather than risk being left out of the team altogether.

I felt like a spare part and hardly seemed to be in the game and was mostly employed as a defender against what was the England-elect side.

Maybe it was a crafty plan to play me in the second

team to test whether my defence was up to it, despite it always being one of my strong points when playing at fly-half.

However, a young flanker by the name of Budge Rogers, who later became president of the RFU, suddenly appeared on the scene in the final trial playing on the same side as me.

'The Rest' were performing very well and giving England a hard time, Richard Sharp was struggling with Budge putting himself about and making things very difficult for him.

Out of the blue at half-time the message came through, 'Sharp off, Risman to move to fly-half in the England team,' that's how things were done then, without ceremony.

After an anxious wait over the weekend, I got the news that Richard had been dropped and I was back in the team against South Africa.

Richard sent me a letter of congratulation, a wonderful and appreciated gesture and I was subsequently delighted that he went on to fulfil his potential by becoming a British Lion.

During all this time, Dad was keeping me informed on the rugby league front and that clubs were monitoring my selection or otherwise.

It was a desperately disappointing England season for me, the first matches against South Africa at Twickenham, lost 5-0 and Wales in Cardiff, which saw us defeated 6-3, were played in mud baths.

Reports suggested that I played well but our forwards were overpowered.

Then came Ireland at Lansdowne Road. We had three quality centres vying for places in Bill Patterson, Malcolm Phillips and Mike Weston.

Bill and Mike had been chosen against South Africa and Malcolm was restored for the Welsh match at the expense of Bill.

Come the Irish and the selectors made six changes.

Budge replaced Peter Robbins for his first cap, David Marques and John Curry, after almost a lifetime together in the second row, were both dropped and replaced by Ray French and John Price. Malcolm Philipps was surprisingly left out with me at centre and Richard returning at fly-half, the failed experiment was being re-tried against a side going for the Triple Crown.

All the pundits said the England selectors had been very brave and changes had to be made but there was some mixed opinion about my selection at centre.

There were a few uncomplimentary comments about me not big or fast enough, having a suspect defence and being more suited as an alternative full-back.

As it turned out, it was a magnificent match played in good conditions and my most rewarding in an England shirt despite being such underdogs.

We lost 11-8 in the end but gave Ireland a real fright coming back from 11 points down to within inches of victory.

Dickie Jeeps and Richard Sharp played well in the halves and our three-quarters had plenty of running opportunities.

Despite my initial reservations about centre, I found that there was often more space than at fly-half and, with more one-on-one's, it was possible to take on my opposite number with some success and I had a good game against my old Lions mate David Hewitt.

Although we lost, the press was quite complimentary about our performance and the selectors made only one change for the following match against France.

Chaired by Carson Catcheside, and including my old friend Mickey Steele Bodger, they ignored the growing rumours of my apparent defection to rugby league.

Once more, on a crucial occasion for me, the weather intervened for the worst and the pitch at Twickenham was in a mess.

The wind was blowing and the surface boggy after incessant rain, negating the open game that both sides preferred to play.

As a result, my future career was decided after this match.

I hardly received a pass for the whole time as I aimlessly chased kicks by both France and England in a dreary, mistake-riddled five-all draw.

It was so disappointing after the performance in Ireland and deeply frustrating for me to have virtually no opportunity to make any sort of contribution.

There was one more match to go against Scotland and some calls for me to be restored to fly-half but there was only one change to the line-up, and I was dropped.

Maybe if I had been selected in my rightful role I might never have crossed the Rubicon, but I doubt it.

On reflection, I have a feeling that the union selectors had come to the conclusion that I was on my way to league and was just playing out the season.

Negotiations had been going on for some time but I had made no promises to anyone and it was only when we reached the last International that I was actually able to make up my mind.

Being left out of the team against the Scots accelerated my decision and instead of facing them, I would be pulling on the red and white hoops of Leigh instead.

I kept in day to day contact with my father who had

been dealing with the Leigh chairman Jack Harding, and being left out of the England team was the clincher.

Suddenly it was all systems go. I made the decision on Tuesday, signed the forms at a meeting in Derby, trained with my new team on Thursday and was ready to play against Liverpool City on the Saturday.

I was incredibly excited by the prospect although, initially, secrets had to be kept.

There was little news in the press and I had said nothing to my mates at Loughborough as things at the college carried on as normal. I wasn't really prepared for all the furore when the signing was announced.

My fellow students decided it was cause for celebration so I went out and bought a large barrel of beer and festivities continued well into the night.

When I arrived at my parent's home on the East Lancs Road in Worsley, the phone was red hot with congratulations from family, friends and league supporters and words of warning from some of my old union pals.

I couldn't believe that there was so much interest both locally and nationally. The rugby union scribes centred on the fact that I had been dropped from England and I was pleased to see that the majority felt that I had been badly treated.

The rugby league journos made a meal of the apparent world record signing-on fee, previously held by Lewis Jones, and were full of comparisons with my dad.

He turned professional in 1928 for £100 paid in instalments, my fee was sixty times that amount, I had a lot to live up to!

Plenty of people thought I'd never be as good as he was, some had already decided I wouldn't make it, and there was debate about my best position speculating between stand-off and full-back, centre was never mentioned.

None of this was helping my nerves and, as Saturday approached, I was more apprehensive than I can ever remember.

Liverpool were not particularly strong, expectations were high and it was important that I put in a good performance on my debut, where I would be a marked man.

I had only one training session and despite having watched rugby league all my life, I was very naive about the skills and technicalities of the professional game.

I'd no idea about the standard of play especially positionally, or the sheer speed of running and handling.

I was also concerned about the physicality of the sport which I thought was often quite brutal.

It was an integral part of the game in those days and you had to keep an eye open for the 'silent assassins.'

Derek Hurt, who I went to school with in Cockermouth, said that he would look after me along with another of the Leigh hard men, Stan Owen.

They were so successful that I was hardly touched for most of the game apart from having to make an occasional tackle and one significant incident.

It was well past the half way mark of the season and there were about ten matches left for me to find my feet but nothing seemed to matter except this one match.

I felt as though I had the whole world on my shoulders as the moment arrived.

A couple of weeks previously, I'd played in front of 70,000 spectators at Twickenham but that seemed to be nothing compared with the 7,500 who packed into Hilton Park.

The papers were full of the story, suddenly I was the man of the moment with every journalist trying to get his own angle.

Mum and Dad were both interviewed. Dad was quite circumspect, saying that I had the makings of a fine player and Mum was most happy that I had secured my financial future.

Ann was tracked down in Cumberland where she was teaching in Workington and had her photo taken in her academic gown.

The immortal Eddie Waring, the voice of league with pen and microphone, made much of my fee and observed that I was only the sixth England union international to turn professional, following on from the likes of Jim Brough, Pat Quinn and Martin Regan, one of my predecessors at fly-half.

There were articles from all the rugby league writers of the day, great names such as Joe Humphries, Jack Bentley, David Short, Jack McNamara and John Bapty, all pontificating about my likely success or failure.

If only we had such coverage filling all the national newspapers today and keeping the sport in the headlines.

Jack Harding and his fellow directors had shown much faith and enterprise and despite the fact that they had forked out an unprecedented amount of money for my signing, had indicated that up to a further £25,000 could be invested in the team, and I was delighted to be part of that search for success.

I still found it difficult to accept that my rugby union days were now behind me but when match day arrived there were no regrets and I felt fully focussed on my new career.

I was in peak condition as a result of my PE course at Loughborough and regular training and playing right up to the week before my Leigh debut.

I set off for Hilton Park from my Mum and Dad's house in my little Austin van in good time for the five mile journey.

I'd only met my new team mates at training on the Thursday night but I was welcomed enthusiastically.

The first thing that struck me in the cramped changing room was the different atmosphere and attitudes of the players compared with rugby union.

Professional was the word, and everything was deadly serious with the pre-match ritual all about personal preparation.

Each player had their own routine, strapping and massage by the physio with help from the reserves and, as kick off drew near, their preferred warm up.

There was none of the hysterical thrashing, bashing, cursing and shouting which was typical of a union changing room, some of the Leigh lads just sat and contemplated until they heard the referee's whistle.

I was never part of the head banging brigade, I had my own stretching exercises and swig of sherry for last minute stimulation.

A final word from Jack Helme our coach: "Get f...ing stuck in," and we were on the field.

Our forwards were formidable, as strong as any in the league, with wily and respected Wally Tabern at hooker, mobile and massive Bill Robinson and the terrifying Welshman Stan Owen as our props.

In the back-row, Mick Martyn, arguably the fastest forward in the game and a prolific try scorer and two ball players, Derek Hurt and Don Platt.

In the backs, we had the reliable John Chadwick, and on the wings ace sidestepper Tony Leadbetter, another union signing, and speedster Jim Humble.

In the centre was a quality rugby union star from Wales, Gordon Lewis and young and talented local lad Ray Fisher.

My partner at half-back was human dynamo Brian Brooks who combined his duties at scrum-half by playing as an extra forward.

It was, potentially, a squad as strong as any.

Despite warnings that I should keep a low profile in the early stages, I was determined to make an impact right from the start.

Everything went serenely as we built up a good lead, I made a couple of good breaks and had a hand in two of our tries. I shared the goal kicking with Don Platt and, after an early miss which gave me a few butterflies, I was relieved to pop over my first goal in my new environment.

I hardly had a tackle to make as our forwards took a firm grip and I was able to concentrate solely on attack.

Eventually, when we had taken full control and had the game virtually won, my bodyguard, Derek Hurt gave me the perfect chance to show my skills.

He whispered to me: "Come off my left shoulder this time," took the ball in at first receiver, ran at a ragged defence and put me through a gap that you could drive a bus through.

I took his short pass on the run and darted into open space with no one but Ray Ashby the Liverpool custodian blocking my way to the line.

This was my moment to make a statement so instead of passing the ball, I decided to take Ray on with a side step.

It seemed to work perfectly as he was wrong-footed and headed towards the terraces as I went the other way.

My head came up as I looked towards the try line only to find that his right arm came round and pole-axed me with an impact right across the nose.

That's all I remember, I was out like a light, and the home crowd were baying for his blood.

On came our physio, Bill Hughes who smashed me in the face with his magic sponge.

As I came round and staggered groggily to my feet, he assured me firmly that I was okay.

Then somewhere in the distance, I heard Stan Owen comforting me with the words: "Never mind, boyo, we got two points for the penalty."

We were already 20 points up and didn't really need them as the union star was led to the touchline, my nose has never been the same.

Ray went on to play full back for Wigan and Great Britain and when I met him socially in the bar at a game in Widnes fifty years later, he rushed across, grinning broadly and said: "I didn't mean it Bev, it was an accident."

We both laughed at the memory but, irrespective, I learned a valuable lesson that first afternoon.

Overall, my debut had worked out well.

The match was well documented in the *Leigh Journal* by Jack Bainbridge, who followed my time there from start to finish. He was a great supporter of Leigh but also a sound and fair judge and I had great respect for his opinions.

I still had to wait for the scrutiny of my most important critics, Mum and Ann had been at the match and Ann was horrified at the incident.

As my greatest supporter, she never got used to seeing me being carted off the field with an injury.

Mum had seen it all before having watched Dad perform for twenty-five years, so was more concerned with how I had played.

Dad, unfortunately, had to attend to his duties as manager of Oldham but was pleased to hear that, apart from a few bumps and bruises, I had come through with some success.

He was getting near to celebrating his 50th Birthday and it was difficult to comprehend that he was still playing at the highest level only six season before.

Once all the excitement had died down, we had to start planning for the remainder of the season.

We had nine matches left and I had to combine training and playing at Leigh with my studies at Loughborough, which meant a lot of travelling up and down the A6.

Hopes were high for a possible place in the play offs and there is no doubt that the team was playing well enough.

We went on a great run as I settled in and finished the season in style with seven victories and only two narrow defeats against top teams Warrington and Swinton.

We just failed to make the top four but there was a feelgood factor after our 46-16 win against Rochdale to end the season, and we couldn't wait for the start of pre-season training in mid-July

In the Doldrums

8

I received my first pay packet on the Thursday after the Liverpool match.

Apart from a few casual holiday jobs, I'd survived on student grants and my parents' generosity and it came as a shock when I realised that I now had to start earning a living.

You might imagine that I'd just pocketed a considerable sum for sacrificing my amateur status as a rugby player so I had no worries.

But I'd not come to terms yet with how this tax-free gift would affect my life as I looked at my first week's wages.

We made eight pounds for winning and would have received three had we lost.

I suddenly had a number of life changing decisions to make as the season came to a close and I completed my course at Loughborough.

I was set to qualify as a teacher in June and had to get a job.

My signing on fee would be invested in bricks and mortar, a new car and preparing myself for a wedding and married life.

I could not rely on the weekly rugby money for very long, and so it proved.

After our winning run up to the end of the 1960-61 season, optimism was high, I'd been able to settle in with few concerns and learned much with every match.

Ann and I fixed our wedding day for 22 July 1961, just after she had completed her first year as a teacher at Workington Grammar School and as pre-season training at Leigh commenced.

She obviously had to resign and find a new job while, luckily for me, a PE job came up at Leigh Grammar School and I was scheduled start in September.

We found a semi-detached house in a cul-de-sac looking out onto Leigh Cricket ground and the local tennis club so everything was falling into place.

The club was generous enough to allow us a two week honeymoon so I would get back in time for the rest of the forthcoming season's preparations.

To complete the jigsaw, Ann got a job teaching English and Drama at Rivington and Blackrod Grammar School and was taken on to start right away.

As far as the rugby was concerned, Leigh never quite got it right over the next four years and we staggered from crisis to crisis both on and off the field.

Don't get me wrong, despite a number of personal difficulties due to injury, I enjoyed my time there and had some success.

I took over the captaincy but we just couldn't get it together for any length of time and while I was there did not win a trophy.

Jack Harding, vice chairman Ken Fletcher, secretary Tom Hourigan and the rest of the board tried every initiative in the search for success but failed in the end.

Successive coaches Jack Helme, Alan Prescott and Gerry Helme worked their socks off but did not seem to have the ability or charisma to get the best out of the playing squad.

Our most high profile coach was Alan Prescott, a legend as a player for St Helens and former Great Britain captain, leading the Lions to victory in Australia in 1958, when he played most of the Second Test with a broken arm.

He always led from the front on the field but despite all his efforts, he was unable to transfer those qualities to his players as a coach.

We failed to produce any level of consistency despite brief periods when we put together a winning streak, all of which caused great frustration amongst directors, coaches, players and supporters, which regularly boiled over.

The supporters blamed the directors, they blamed the coaches who either resigned or were sacked and the coaches blamed the players.

Players came and went, got injured, asked for transfers or just made excuses, it wasn't a recipe for success and there was too much on-going controversy.

The directors and fans were passionate about their club and living in the shadow of Wigan made their thirst for success even greater.

When I signed professional, I was assured by the board that they would leave no stone unturned to get trophies in the cabinet.

The certainly tried but apart from one appearance in the Lancashire Cup final which was lost against St Helens and some Mackeson Trophy tankards, we won nothing.

Jack and his cohorts dug deep into their pockets and made a number of high profile signings including Danny Harris, the Welsh rugby union second rower, who arrived to great acclaim.

A giant of a man with pace and skills, he didn't seem to have the temperament and, for whatever reason, never really achieved the prowess of which he was capable and finished up on the transfer list, quite disillusioned.

Three South Africans with good reputations, backs Ken Bounzier, Chris Lansberg and goal-kicking full-back Piet Botha came and went in very short time.

Mick Murphy and Mike Collins arrived also from union and became stalwarts but could not seem to make the essential difference to bring success.

Experienced, quality rugby league players Austin Rhodes, Ken Large, Geoff Fletcher and others were signed but silverware continued to elude us.

Then the money started to run out and the club had to be bolstered by a substantial donation from the ever-faithful supporters club to recruit even more players.

Local talent such as Rodney Tickle and Ian Hodgkiss, arguably the fastest winger in the game, was nurtured and young forwards like Stan Walmsley, Bob Welding and Derek Higgs were given a chance, but still the right combination proved impossible to find.

Our trusted forwards Stan Owen, Wally Tabern, Bill Robinson, Mick Martyn – perhaps the only one who stood the test of time while I was there – and Derek Hurt gradually lost their power as they aged.

Stan was a tower of strength with the ball in his hands often looking to take on the whole of the opposition as he deftly slipped the ball to a supporting player, usually Mick.

But he was a liability in defence as he seemed

determined to be sent off with virtually every tackle he made as his red mist frequently descended.

The legend goes that he only ever made 18 tackles and was sent off 18 times, he seemed to spend more time at the disciplinary than on the pitch.

I had my own ups and downs, gave decent service despite the injuries, played as many matches as any of the other and as captain, was as passionate as anyone for the club to be successful.

I was in the national selectors' minds on a number of occasions and had spells when I was getting good reports whether I was playing at stand-off, my preferred position, full-back the one which several judges saw suited me best, or even occasional centre, as required.

I got close to a Great Britain call up at stand-off but was competing against then current greats Dave Bolton, Alan Hardisty and the mercurial Alex Murphy.

I did, however, feature for a representative team made of ex rugby union players for a match against France in Paris, played under experimental rules in which the ball had to be released in the tackle.

During my time as a player there was always controversy about the best way to restart after a tackle and over the years there were several changes to the rule, mainly in an attempt to open up the game and produce a faster and more exciting spectacle.

I believe we've now got it right with the six-tackle rule, although having also played under four that produced some incredible passages of play but proved to be just too fast for some teams.

The Paris match produced total mayhem with the ball flying about all over the place and a mass of scrums.

Needless to say, although the proposal was dropped,

we enjoyed a great weekend in the French capital. Many, including journalist Jack McNamara, thought I was best suited to full-back and even Dad agreed.

My appearances there for Leigh were always temporary and although I produced some of my best performances in the role, it always seemed to be as cover.

During a longer spell in the number one shirt, my name was put forward for Great Britain alongside Swinton's Ken Gowers who had been a fixture in the international side for a number of years.

It did not materialise, however, as I got injured before the series against New Zealand and was not available for selection anyway.

Perhaps I was rather obstinate about changing to full-back because I wanted to prove myself at the highest level in my noted position of stand-off and those proposing that I should change tended to give negative reasons for it citing, "he needs more room to exploit his skills," or even worse, "he lacks a yard of pace."

I never accepted those criticisms but even Eddie Waring had his say during the course of one of his commentaries when he came out with the now infamous comment: "That Risman, he is deceptively slow."

We settled into life in Leigh. Ann and I were enjoying it, we'd made some good friends at the club and elsewhere when suddenly we were hit with a double whammy.

Before the start of the 1962-63 season, we had been away on holiday in France and I returned bronzed and fit before the annual charity game against Widnes.

I'd been in full training prior to the break and got back on the Thursday, originally not being required to play but there was a last minute cry-off so I was thrown back in at the deep end.

During the match, Widnes winger Johnny Gaydon ran clear and I rushed across to tackle him.

Being a friendly, neither of us wanted to be involved in any major heroics but we both had to go through the motions.

He slowed down and hoped for an easy run in and I made a half-hearted tackle and mistimed it completely.

I don't know exactly what happened but the next thing I remember was Bill Hughes, our celebrated physio, hitting me in the face with a wet sponge.

There was blood all over it but he was telling me I was fine to carry on.

It was only when I was called upon to take a penalty and started to kick the ball in the wrong direction that it was realised something was seriously wrong.

I was carted off with severe concussion, eventually taken to hospital being sick all over Ken Fletcher's car on the way, and was immediately operated on for a complicated fracture of the jaw.

A week or so later, Ann developed morning sickness, an unmistakable sign that our first child was on the way.

I had my jaws clamped together and could not eat solid food, and she didn't want to eat anything at all, at least it kept the housekeeping bills down.

I went back to my teaching job trying to talk without opening my mouth, my students in 4C having a whale of a time at my expense.

Martin, the first of our three sons, was born in Leigh in March '63 and apart from a rocky start necessitating an operation on his stomach, he soon developed into a real livewire.

I couldn't wait to teach him how to catch, pass, punt and sidestep.

Ann and I continued to enjoy our social life. I kept in contact with several of my old union pals despite the taboo operated by the RFU at the time for, apparently, selling my soul.

Players from both codes seemed to get on well together and I would occasionally have a beer, go to a party or attend a union match without any conflict.

Only occasionally was I confronted and would usually walk away but I never accepted being exiled or the ridiculous prejudice that accompanied such an attitude, I was determined to attempt to sit on both sides of the fence.

There was one occasion, though, not long after I joined Leigh when I was invited to a fancy dress party by Broughton Park rugby union club.

It had come specifically from Mike O'Donnell, one of my university friends who also played on the wing for Lancashire at the same time I did.

I knew quite a few of the lads there such as Peter and Geoff Barrett and Barry Jackson, so was delighted to accept.

Ann and I got all dolled up in Hawaiian outfits and took Derek Hurt and his wife Pat along with us to provide moral support.

We were made thoroughly welcome by the members of the club and were enjoying an entertaining evening when who should turn up but the Lancashire RFU party fresh from a defeat at Durham earlier in the day.

I'd had three seasons playing for the red rose and knew most of the players very well and we were quite prepared for plenty of socialising when, after a few behind the scenes mutterings, I was told by one of the Lancashire officials that it was not appropriate for us to be present and we should leave.

I politely pointed out that we'd been officially invited

and it should be up to the Broughton Park club to decide whether we stayed or not.

I told Mike and the club officials what had happened and, to their credit, they backed me up and said that if anyone should leave it should be the Lancashire party who had not been invited in the first place.

Rather than it prove an extremely embarrassing incident for the club, I decided that we should strategically withdraw.

It transpired that the issue revolved around Tom Brophy, who had taken over from me in the Lancashire team.

He was the subject of rumours flying around that he was about to sign professional and they thought I might be encouraging him to do so.

Tom did eventually sign for Barrow but it was certainly nothing to do with me.

Naturally, I have to accept that rugby union in Lancashire did lose many outstanding players to league over the years so I can perhaps understand the sensitivity of the Lancashire officials.

High profile players such as Bill Burgess and my old mate Ray French 'defected', as well as my colleagues at Leigh, Tony Leadbetter, Mike Collins and Mick Murphy.

My pal from Manchester University days Dave Parker signed for Oldham and went on to play for Great Britain in 1964 against France.

You must choose one or the other was the rule but one of the biggest anomalies in the rugby apartheid debate involved Ray French and I throughout our playing days.

Despite being occasionally ostracised, we were able to continue our links with rugby union in the school environment.

Ray was a teacher at Cowley and part of his duties

was coaching union while still playing league for St Helens and later Widnes.

I was able to operate in the same way at Leigh GS and later Bradford Grammar, none of the private schools offering league, not surprisingly.

It would have been great to teach both sports openly but, unfortunately at that time, any of our boys who wanted to play league could only do so in their own time for amateur clubs.

To play 13-a-side they had to attend a secondary modern or one of the new comprehensives, times have changed, fortunately.

Ray and I had parallel careers, we have never seemed to be far from one another, which led to an enduring friendship.

"Though I have never been persuaded to visit a psychiatrist, the feeling of being followed has been with me throughout the whole of my career in rugby," Ray confirms.

"And I am sure that my good friend Bev has suffered from similar inclinations whenever he has glanced at a team sheet, read a match report in the newspapers or listened to an announcement on league or union matters on TV or radio.

"For, unlike any other double act in either code, our careers have intertwined with uncanny regularity both on and off the pitch."

He adds: "Whether as a student representing the English Universities at rugby union, playing for Lancashire in the county championship, battling against the might of South Africa for the North West Counties at Maine Road, Manchester, or running onto the pitch at Twickenham in an England jersey, the names of Risman and French were prominent together in the programmes.

"And, lo and behold, we decided to switch codes

within a week of each other and for as long as I can remember, have enjoyed each other's company in the boardroom or on the touchline and I have always been grateful for his sound advice.

"Though unassuming and quiet off the pitch, Bev was a firm leader on it with the natural footballing skills and shrewd tactical knowledge which, in whatever team he played at club or international level, naturally elevated him to the position of captain.

"In an era when a captain did not receive advice on the field from a water bottle carrier or had tactics relayed to him via a walkie-talkie system but was in complete charge, he was in control at all times and ever sympathetic to the views and aspirations of all around him.

"Over the past 50-odd years he has proved to be a beacon of good sense and a presence for enlightened change both on and off the pitch."

Time for a Change

9

My first five years as a professional were very tough, but it was a worthwhile experience that taught me a lot.

I made nearly 150 appearances for Leigh in all and scored over 600 points, my last full season for them in 1964-65 was my best-ever with 36 appearances and 105 goals.

Yet the team had little success. Life was a rollercoaster of limited triumph and frequent disappointment.

At 28, my time for representative honours was running out but my ambition to represent my country at rugby league was as intense as ever.

My rugby career seemed to be grinding to a halt and I could not see my way forward, I had given everything I could to Leigh so the best option was to ask for a transfer and make a new start.

Things had looked so different at the start of the 1963-64 campaign, we were in Division 2 and expected to get promoted.

I was settled at full-back and the side was undefeated in eight matches, including a sensational win at derby rivals Wigan in the Lancashire Cup.

It was the best result in any game I played for Leigh but unfortunately I received a serious injury to my left knee which was to affect the rest of my time in the sport.

Trevor Lake, Wigan's South African winger, was diving for the line and I slid in under him to try to prevent the score.

As he threw himself down on my outstretched leg, I felt my knee collapse under his body weight.

I hated showing that I was injured so I got up immediately and attempted to stand but the knee kept giving way, I even limped to the half way line to take the kick off.

But, when I tried to swing my leg, it was as though there was nothing there below my knee.

I had to be helped off the field to eventually find that I had seriously damaged my knee ligaments and would be out of commission for several weeks.

Young Colin Tyrer, who had been showing tremendous promise, was able to take over the role.

My move to full-back had meant that he was missing out or playing on the wing and getting increasingly frustrated, and had asked for a transfer.

He performed brilliantly for several weeks as Leigh continued their successful spell and eventually had a top career at Wigan.

My form at the time was such that I was tipped to challenge Ken Gowers for the Great Britain full-back spot in the forthcoming Tests against Australia but, again, bad timing.

I was frantic to get fit again but the injury was quite serious.

Even so, I targeted a return for the Lancashire Cup final against favourites St Helens.

It was a big mistake, I was obviously not fully fit but under pressure to play because it was such a big match.

I did, we lost 15-4 and I was given a hard time by the local press, understandably because I'd had a poor game due to lack of fitness.

We started to lose our form and were sliding down the table, our only real chance of glory had gone and I felt I'd let everyone down by playing when I shouldn't have.

It was a situation I'd experienced a number of times in the past and sometimes taken the chance and got away with it, on this occasion, I'd gambled and lost.

The plummet in form, which was affecting our chances of promotion, caused problems at the club and someone had to pay, somewhat surprisingly, Alan Prescott was sacked.

I continued to play on despite problems with my knee and was performing poorly.

Gerry Helme took over temporarily as coach, my knee was getting no better and further damage caused me to miss more matches.

There was increasing unrest, unhappy players and transfer requests, the club had lost all sense of direction.

I continued to play below par as the knee was just not right, the problem had gone on for nearly three months and I was starting to feel as though it was permanently damaged.

I kept breaking down in matches and it would become swollen, I almost felt as if I was running on one leg.

I went to see a specialist who decided that the knee had completely seized up and needed a manipulative operation, it was my own fault for continuing to play when I was probably not fit.

It was a low point for me and I was starting to think that my professional playing days might be over.

Gerry was appointed coach on a full-time basis and I came back from a rest after my operation determined that I would concentrate on helping the club out in whatever way I could until the end of the season.

I played anywhere, the knee was slowly getting stronger and in the Challenge Cup we had something of a saga with Widnes which required two replays to settle the tie.

Sadly, we lost and to rub it in I missed vital goals in the second replay which could have given us a famous victory but I was just happy to get to the end of the season.

I played with heavy strapping on in every match but was delighted that the knee stayed intact, give or take a few wobbles, for the rest of my career.

I had trained hard in the close season and at long last was back in excellent condition but the 1964-5 season at Hilton Park illustrated my dilemma.

With the championship reverting to one division and more top teams to face, we started disastrously, losing our first nine matches and I was moved about in three different positions but was in a good vein of form.

Things started to click for the side and I settled back into my normal role at stand-off as we won nine out of ten matches and I was being talked about once again as a potential international.

The annual fixtures against France were coming up in December 1964 and the following January but I wasn't holding my breath.

Although Dave Bolton's brilliant career was coming to an end, I still had to contend with established stars Frank Myler and Alex Murphy.

Murphy was an outstanding player, probably the

greatest half-back of all time in my opinion but he was controversial and not always flavour of the month with the selectors.

Ken Gowers had locked up the full-back position and rapidly emerging Alan Hardisty had been the selectors' choice at stand-off the previous season.

In the event I was chosen as a reserve for the match in Perpignan, presumably because of my utility value but this was at a time when substitutes could only replace an injured player and neither of us got the chance to enter the fray.

We shuffled our feet in vain on the touchline itching to get on while not really wanting anyone to get hurt.

Despite being favourites, Great Britain went down to an unexpected 18-8 defeat but I was not selected even as reserve for the return match and there were no further fixtures until the Tests against New Zealand the next autumn.

It seemed as though my international career was over before it had begun but I was at least enjoying my rugby again.

Leigh signed experienced Austin Rhodes from St Helens, a quality player who like me didn't receive as many caps as he might have done because he shone in more than one position. We struck up a great partnership, not everything was plain sailing, though, as we lost at home to Bradford in the Challenge Cup.

By then, Dad was manager of Northern – I never did manage to put one over on him!

We went undefeated for the last six matches of the regular season and got into the play-offs by beating Warrington in the last game.

Unfortunately, they reversed the result in the first round and although desperately disappointed, the club at least seemed to be in better shape.

A bigger personal thrill was becoming a father for the second time when son John arrived on 27 March 1965.

Ann had decided to have the baby at home and I was intending to be at the birth, quite an experience in those days, although being a biology teacher, I thought I could handle it.

The time duly arrived and the midwife was called on the evening of 26 March.

We were due to play at Whitehaven the next day, a five hour trip starting from Hilton Park at the crack of dawn.

Ann really tried her best but John did not arrive until the early hours of the morning.

We'd already agreed that I would play providing everything went alright with the birth.

It was brilliant, one of the greatest experiences of my life and Ann was a heroine, baby and mother were both fine but I was mentally exhausted.

Still, she insisted that everything was under control so, having had no sleep, I staggered off to meet the bus in the early hours of the morning.

I felt I could not let the club or the team down even though I was in no state to put in any sort of a performance but thankfully we won 7-2 and I kicked two goals with my eyes barely open.

Come the '65-6 season and Jack Rubin had taken over as Leigh chairman from Jack Harding and arrived all guns blazing demanding open attractive rugby.

Competition for places was high and we even had trial matches. Everyone was really excited about our prospects but again things did not go well.

We made a terrible start and lost the first five matches and unrest quickly set in.

Transfer requests were submitted including from Austin Rhodes who was quickly snapped up by Swinton,

Geoff Fletcher who went to Oldham, while Gordon Lewis and John Lewis also wanted to leave.

There was even an unsubstantiated rumour that there was an approach for me from Workington and that I would be on my way back to Cumberland because my wife was unhappy.

It was all rubbish but I had to start assessing my options, Leigh were in the doldrums again and we had seen it all before.

As usual I kept my head down but I could see my career slipping away if I didn't do something drastic.

I was still in the frame for international selection and was on a list of early nominees for the Australian Tour in summer 1966 and before that, the Kiwis were coming over.

After much soul searching, I decided to ask for a transfer, the local press was full of it and demanded an explanation.

Initially I refused to be drawn into a long and complicated discussion about my reasons but after a short period of silence, I decided that it would be for the best if I made a statement after the club had agreed to my request.

I was placed on the list at £9,500, a ridiculous figure that no club could afford. Money was tight in the game at that time so there was no likelihood of a move at that price.

Perhaps Leigh calculated that I would have second thoughts and the figure would persuade me to stay if no-one came up with an offer but my mind was made up.

I continued to play but in such circumstances you are in a no man's land and, whatever your intentions, it is impossible to do yourself justice and the best for the team while also trying to attract other clubs.

I was kidding myself really and had to recognise that there was no chance of representative selection while I was at loggerheads with Leigh. As time went on, I started to question if I had done the right thing.

Matches came and went and then disaster struck, after a long injury-free period, my left knee went again and I lost the final chance of selection for Great Britain that late autumn.

It was somewhat ironic that when the team for the First Test against New Zealand was announced, there was no Hardisty or Murphy and, out of the blue, Whitehaven's Phil Kitchen was chosen at stand-off with Tommy Smales from Featherstone as captain and his partner in the halves.

Phil was a good friend of mine and I was delighted he got his chance because he was a great player and his selection was fully deserved, but I could not help thinking that I could have been there.

As Phil won his first cap, so did Paul Charlton from Workington who was to become one of the great full-backs and I was delighted that my team mate at Leigh, Gordon Lewis was also selected.

It felt like a new era but I was still on the outside.

Despite the injury, I never thought of retiring and was determined to get back on the field either with Leigh or with another club as soon as possible, I had to just dig in and work hard to get fit again.

In the meantime, I was really thankful that I had my family, Ann was a tower of strength looking after me and our two young sons and I was able to spend more time with them, also keep myself busy with my teaching job at Leigh Grammar School.

I asked Leigh to lower my transfer fee, they realised that I was still determined to leave and make a fresh start so they agreed, dropping it to £7,000, still a massive amount for a player who was on the sidelines.

Dad set the ball rolling by making a bid for me to sign for Bradford Northern as I returned to the team but it was rejected then, at last, there was an offer from Leeds.

Joe Warham had nearly signed me five years earlier for the Loiners when they required a goal-kicking full-back and their coach Roy Francis had suggested that I might be the man.

Now, Ken Thornett, their outstanding Kangaroo full-back was returning home and Robin Dewhurst, who Leeds had been grooming to take his place, had just been seriously injured, coincidentally with an identical injury to mine.

Leeds needed an immediate replacement and I would be required to play exclusively at full-back and be responsible for the kicking duties.

Joe takes up the story. "We initially met when I was playing for Swinton and living not far from the Manchester University playing fields as Bev's renown was beginning to emerge.

"I meandered there occasionally to see how the son of Gus was measuring up to the legacy bequeathed to him. It was very evident that the succession was to be a happy one.

"We tried to sign him before he went to Leigh but in many discussions at Gus's pub on the border of Yorkshire and Lancashire, he made it clear that he thought it a little crazy on our part to talk about the current highly successful England union stand-off signing for Leeds as a full-back.

"My plea that a lack of blistering pace was less vital to the full-back was met with derision."

As Leeds's manager, Joe continued to keep a watch on me.

"Bev didn't explode, he glided into the attack with all the smoothness, almost languor, of true artistry – he wasn't slow and was probably much faster than he looked.

"And when we finally got our man, it was one of the best deals ever."

I would have to uproot the family and get a new full-time job but this was the chance I had longed for.

In our good run the season before, Leigh's only defeat had been against Leeds at Hilton Park, winger Ronnie Cowan had scored a hat trick that day, joining after playing rugby union for Scotland and the British Lions.

Ann and I became good friends with Ron and his wife Gladys and he has told me many a story about his initial exile following a lifetime ban from any connection with union in the country of his birth, which was quite shameful.

I really felt that this would be my last and best chance to scale the heights in rugby league, Ann and I agreed that we should go for it and try to rescue my career.

The clubs negotiated a transfer fee and I will be forever grateful to the Leigh Directors for their generosity and understanding at a very difficult time for me.

People say that there is no room for sentiment in sport and often tough decisions have to be made as a consequence.

On this occasion, with the help and goodwill of Leigh and the willingness of Leeds to take a chance on an ageing, injury-prone utility player, I was rescued from potential oblivion.

A New World

10

As a rugby union player I'd been extremely fortunate to experience the best that the amateur game had to offer, with all the five star luxury treatment that went with being an England international and British Lion.

As a part-time rugby league player with Leigh in the hard-bitten environment of the professional game, I spent five years learning my trade and biding my time.

It had been a demanding but rewarding experience and I thought that I now knew what the sport was all about but it had almost brought me to, and cost me, my knees.

The difference at Leeds, though, could not have been more marked to that at Leigh.

From the moment I arrived at Headingley, I immediately felt at home in the magnificent facilities of the combined cricket and rugby, dual Test complex.

The rugby section was administered like a well-oiled machine with no stone unturned to provide the best possible environment for all concerned, especially the players - they could have no excuses to perform.

Jack Myerscough, the chairman, was a successful Yorkshire businessman who called a spade a spade but ruled the club with an iron fist.

General manager Alf Rutherford was the epitome of efficiency, he looked after the players as if they were the crown jewels and did not hesitate to get out the champagne in the players' bar after we had delivered a particularly spectacular win and that was quite frequently.

No wonder that Leeds were called the aristocrats of the sport especially as entrepreneur Noel Stockdale, a senior member of the board and long-time supporter of the club with his family, provided financial stability to an already wealthy club.

Our coach was Roy Francis, who played in the same era as my dad. He was a revolutionary thinker about the game, the master of player psychology and a fanatical fitness guru, a visionary far ahead of his time.

Just the man to sort me out, I hoped.

At my first training session, I was met by Arthur Crowther the kit man who ruled the changing room.

He showed me to my peg where my training kit was all laid out; immaculately clean boots and spikes all polished ready for training. It was exactly the same for every session for the next five years, he attended to my every need, even the jockstraps were personalised!

I knew most of my new team mates if not personally at least by reputation, including Harry Poole the captain who went on to be selected for the touring Great Britain Lions later in the season. Roy and Joe had already told me what was expected, but I soon realised that it was much more than that when training began.

The spikes were on as we ventured onto the hallowed cricket field for our Tuesday evening fitness run.

I had always been an enthusiastic and dedicated trainer and with my PE teaching background thought I knew what it was all about, but was not prepared for what was to come as Roy took over.

His philosophy revolved around quality and the development of speed and the whole session was built around improving the players as athletes with exercises to increase flexibility and pace.

Over 50 years ago he was using the training methods prevalent nowadays and there is no doubt that it made a fundamental difference to our performance.

I was nowhere near his required fitness levels and my first few weeks were spent trying to improve my speed and stamina to cope with his demands.

After a series of warm up exercises, Roy would put us into competitive groups with the backs and forwards split.

I was still carrying old wounds and was much slower than the others in mine. Everyone had to reach target times in 150 yard interval runs around the perimeter of the cricket field. Roy deliberately put me with all the fliers; John Atkinson, Alan Smith, Ronnie Cowan, Geoff Wrigglesworth and Mick Shoebottom.

We did 12 interval runs at almost sprinting pace. A different runner would take the lead each time and the rest had to stay as close to him as possible.

In order to try and keep up, I had to sprint full out all the time and when it was my turn to lead I knew that the others were just strolling along behind me.

It was embarrassing but I believe to this day that such arduous work made an enormous difference to my game and all my aches, pains and niggling injuries seemed to disappear.

Over my time at Leeds, I only missed a handful of games. Alan Smith was at my side as I attempted to adapt to the new surroundings and methods.

"Rumours spread fast, players and officials from other clubs would turn up on training nights to witness the relentless sprinting Roy was putting everyone through, all against his stopwatch and clipboard, where he monitored and mixed up the sprint teams so no one could hide, first team and 'A' team squads all together," he remembers.

"The fitness levels of every player were lifted dramatically. Come the 1965-6 season, Roy had added pace to a pack which could run for a full 80 minutes, he had a back line of internationals in Wrigglesworth, Gemmel, Broatch and Cowan, with an up and coming half back pairing of Shoebottom and Seabourne working round the experienced Harry Poole with a clever loose forward in Ray Batten pressing for a first team spot.

"On top of that he had a young back division in the 'A' team pushing the first teamers for selection – Atkinson, Watson, Hynes and yours truly, but, he only had one full-back. Robin Dewhurst, a young, talented, goal kicking full-back, was looking set for a fine career until a terrible knee injury put paid to that.

"Those unfortunate circumstances closed the door on one player's opportunity and sent Leeds out on a mission to open another.

"I'm not sure Bev knew what he was getting into at 28, a glittering rugby union career and Lions tour behind him, and five years playing rugby league with Leigh at stand-off and centre.

"But, he was spared no time for past achievements, straight into a pair of spikes and sprint training the likes of which, I suspect, he had never done before.

"When all around the cricket field were players fighting for air to recover from a completed sprint, Bev had that unnerving air of control, could he go faster? Wingers could never shake him off.

"The foundations were being put down for a further four years in a glittering career for Bev, faster, and I suspect fitter, than he had ever been in his career. Roy's vision to place him at full-back behind an emerging team that could play rugby and move the ball faster than any other club in the league, was the smartest move of all."

In our Thursday sessions, Roy concentrated on quick ball movement whilst encouraging vision, decision making and support play.

He didn't overload the players with complicated set piece strategies and instructed us to keep the ball alive.

Early the following season, with the introduction of the four tackle rule, our style of play was tailor-made for it and the club entered one of the most successful eras in its history, winning the League Leader's trophy four years in succession.

Having taken over 60 years to win their first Championship title under Lewis Jones in 1961, that side had broken up quickly in what had seemed a one-off.

The club was ready for a shake up and performances started to improve again as young local players flourished under the Francis regime.

John Atkinson and Alan Smith dominated the wing position for years, Mick Shoebottom and Barry Seaborne flourished at half-back alongside Ken Rollin who had been tempted from temporary retirement at Wakefield, again Roy mixing youth and experience to great effect so they could bounce off each other.

Syd Hynes ruled the roost in the centre with first of

all Dick Gemmell then Bernard Watson and another Scot Drew Broatch. The core of younger players were joined by experienced and rugged ball playing forwards led by Poole, Mick Clark, Allen Lockwood, Les Chamberlain and South African Louis Neumann.

Magician Ray Batten eventually made the loose-forward position his own, brothers Albert and Ken Eyre, assassin Bill Ramsey and York's flying hooker Tony Crosby all joined the ranks.

Roy was putting together a squad that could handle his style of play and I was signed to fill a hole at the back.

Robin's misfortune gave me a chance and I'm glad that he eventually recovered and was able to play some part in our success before transferring to Bramley.

It was not an easy decision to unsettle my family and make a new life in Yorkshire.

The alternative to moving house and job was to stay in Leigh and travel three or four times a week over the Pennines to Leeds, a journey of four to five hours.

At that stage I had no idea how it would pan out but I was determined take every possible step to ensure success.

I signed for Leeds in early February 1966 and was straight into the team for our home match against Dewsbury.

Initially, I had no option but to travel back and forth because I had to fulfil my teaching commitments at Leigh Grammar School while I looked for a new job and base.

There was no M62 in those days so I had to plough my way over the Pennines on the A628 past the Nont Sarah's pub, which Mum and Dad ran.

It was a very popular stop off for rugby league teams and supporters and, at the same time, Dad was coaching newly resurrected Bradford Northern.

I was incredibly nervous when I made my Leeds

debut, I knew it was make or break, the management was taking a big chance on me, my league career would be defined by this move and I was asking a lot of my family to follow me.

There were also standards to go with the opulent surroundings, Leeds were expected to beat Dewsbury so that give me some confidence and we were never in trouble as Mick Shoebottom destroyed the opposition with a typical all-action performance.

Geoff Wrigglesworth scored all four tries and, after an early miss, I managed to put over three goals.

Of the team that day, only Cowan, Shoebottom and Clark remained during my tenure at Headingley.

Prior to the transfer, Leeds had endured a moderate first half of the season but the bandwagon began to roll and we won 10 matches on the trot, including victories in the Challenge Cup against York and Hull and started to look forward to a triumphant end to the campaign as we moved up the table.

However, we had a major hiccough over Easter, losing all three matches mainly because we were involved in a monumental battle with Warrington in the cup.

After drawing two-all at Wilderspool, we won the replay at Headingley and, in all, played five matches in 13 days. To ease the load, the players were taken away to the Norbreck Hydro in Blackpool to have some rest and recuperation.

We were given permission to let our hair down a little and experience the Rutherford champagne hospitality.

I can't remember too much about it but I am reliably informed that I was inseparable from a large bottle of whisky.

As the campaign continued, I felt more at home with the team and we started our build up to the Cup semi-final against Wigan and the Championship play offs, having qualified in a creditable sixth position.

Wigan were a mighty team with the likes of Billy Boston, Eric Ashton, Trevor Lake, Cliff Hill and Brian McTigue and were on the top of their game.

Leeds hadn't been to Wembley for 10 years and we were underdogs although, with our recently found form, fancying our chances.

What an anti-climax.

The weather was brutal, it was a gluepot of a pitch at Huddersfield, we had no opportunity to open the game up and, most of all, were without our talisman Mick Shoebottom who was out injured. Wigan just closed us out defensively as we failed to adapt to the conditions and Boston got the only try of the match as we lost 7-2.

Our big chance had gone and although we beat Huddersfield in the first round of the play offs, Wigan well and truly put us in our place again in the quarter finals as we ran out of steam at the end of the season.

There was great excitement about the forthcoming tour of Australia and New Zealand that summer.

A few months before I was seen as a has-been, playing the occasional game for Leigh and seeking a transfer.

Then, suddenly, after a few reasonable games for Leeds, I was being tipped as an outsider for a place in the party.

The competition was formidable with established stars in both the full-back and half-back positions.

At custodian, Ken Gowers was still the automatic choice with Arthur Keegan his back up and, amongst the playmakers – still my position of choice – there was a wealth of talent with Alex Murphy, Tommy Bishop, Alan Hardisty and the emerging Roger Millward in contention.

Once again, the selectors turned a blind eye to my claims, Gowers and Keegan got the expected spots but there were surprises in the halves.

Carl Dooler and Tommy Bishop were selected at scrum-half and Alan Hardisty and Willy Aspinall at stand-off with Alex in there to cover every eventuality.

There was still a twist in the tail because Murphy withdrew and my hopes rose again for a last minute call up but Ian Brooke of Wakefield was selected instead.

In the end, Leeds only managed two representatives, Geoff Wrigglesworth on the wing and Poole's well deserved honour as skipper.

There were rumblings in the Leeds camp about the lack of selections with Dick Gemmell and Mick Shoebottom, in particular, unlucky to miss out.

I followed the tour avidly in the press and was pleased to see Brooke fully justifying his selection playing in all five internationals.

A new season brought a fresh start for me in so many ways. We found a house looking out over Baildon Moor and together with Ann and the boys, I was able to settle into our new life. I needed a new teaching job and, out of the blue, I was contacted by Kenneth Robinson, headmaster of the prestigious Bradford Grammar School.

Mr Robinson had interviewed me when I was looking for my first teaching post after leaving college.

He was head of Birkenhead school at the time and said he could offer me a position but not if I turned professional because I would have to work on Saturdays.

He then advised me to take the golden opportunity of a new challenge and financial security of playing league.

I was forever thankful for his sound advice and he also said that if ever he could help me in the future, I should contact him. As it happened, he contacted me when he learned that I had signed for Leeds and would be living near Bradford and offered me the post of director of P.E. and sport at the school, and I didn't hesitate to accept.

BGS was a famous rugby union school, even though many of the pupils were avid supporters of Bradford Northern and I would be responsible for the school teams.

In addition to my PE duties, I was to work with the first XV during the week but was allowed to play for Leeds on Saturdays when they had matches.

My colleague Chris Bradnock, a stalwart union man from Chalfont St. Giles, would take charge of the school team on match days, I was also assisted by Dave Pennington who became a great friend and a Leeds supporter.

There was general unrest in rugby league with dwindling attendances and several proposals were put forward as to how to overcome the problem.

Australia had already introduced a five yard rule at the play-the-ball instead of three, four tackles had been proposed but was initially rejected for the start of the season, Wigan had even suggested a television ban but were over-ruled by the RL Council, and there was also talk of summer rugby.

After an experimental period, there was a general consensus that the four tackle rule was a success and should be fully employed, leading to more spectacular play and high speed action, which was then coupled with the five yard adoption.

There is no doubt that these changes provided the catalyst for the years of success enjoyed by Leeds during the late '60s when they carried all before them.

Things had started to fall into place and after Roy's pre-season boot camp, we were looking forward to the new

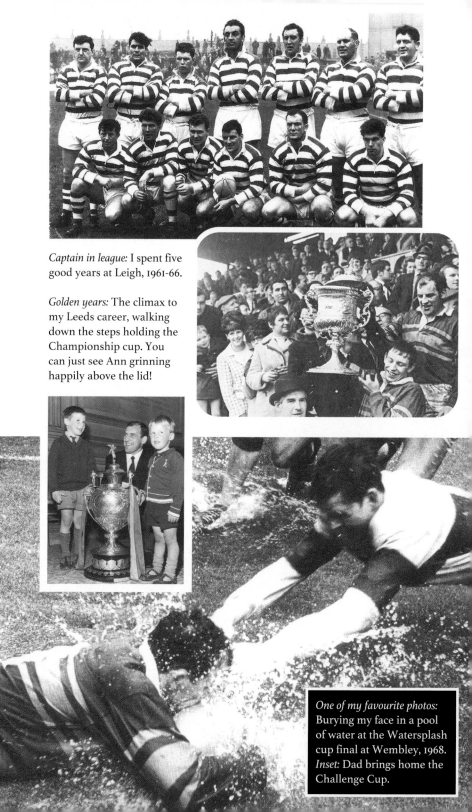

Captain in league: I spent five good years at Leigh, 1961-66.

Golden years: The climax to my Leeds career, walking down the steps holding the Championship cup. You can just see Ann grinning happily above the lid!

One of my favourite photos: Burying my face in a pool of water at the Watersplash cup final at Wembley, 1968. *Inset:* Dad brings home the Challenge Cup.

Full-backs do score tries: Bernard Watson and Leeds winger John Atkinson look on amazed, while, *left*, Barry Seabourne grins as he thinks he's going to beat me in training ... I've got him covered!

Championship final: Versus Castleford at Odsal. Our captain Mick Clark bursts forward with the ball. Ronnie Cowan, *left*, waits for an off-load. I am in the centre, looking on anxiously.

Best year: The most successful team I played with. We won everything in the 1968/69 season. Back: Ken Eyre, Albert Eyre, Mick Clark, Tony Crosby. Ray Batten, Bill Ramsey, Dave Hick, Mick Joyce. Front: Ron Cowan, Bev Risman, Joe Warham (coach), Barry Seaborne, Jack Myerscough (chairman), Bernard Watson, Syd Hynes. Seated on grass: Alan Smith, *left*, Mick Shoebottom, *right*.

Goals aplenty: In action for Leeds, *right*. I was the club's main goal-kicker and top scorer in the league for three seasons.

Just a joke: Having a laugh at the 1968 World Cup in Australia with Kevin Ashcroft, Charlie Renilson, Ian Brook, Tommy Bishop and Chris Young.

Dream come true: Selected for Great Britain. Back: Charlie Renilson, John Warlow, Ray French, Arnie Morgan, Cliff Watson, Bill Francis, Bev Risman. Kneeling: Chris Young, Peter Flanagan, Neil Fox, Tommy Bishop, Roger Millward, Ian Brook.

Above: Captaining Great Britain at Sydney Cricket Ground in 1968, where a record World Cup crowd of 62,256 saw us fall to Australia in game one, 25-10.

Above: A pennant from the World Cup.

End of the World Cup: With 'Flash' Flanagan after victory over the Kiwis, also at the SCG.

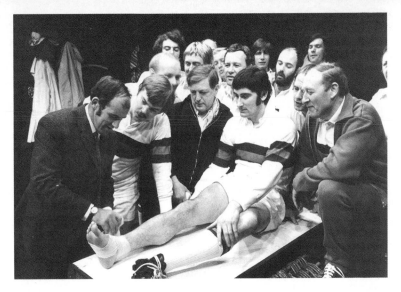

The Changing Room: Acting as advisor to the hugely successful rugby league-based play that ran in London's West End and also on Broadway.

Famous faces: Bumping into fellow British Lions Willie John McBride, John Spencer and Gavin Hastings in South Africa – it may be time for league and union to merge.

Director: In a suit with the London Broncos academy. Third left front row is coach Dave Rotheram.

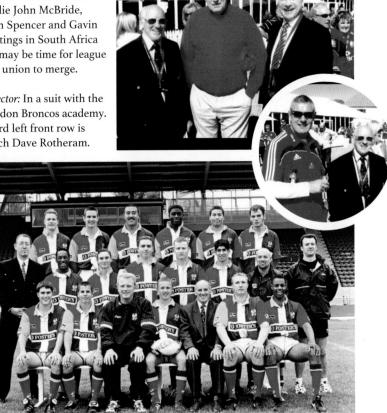

Gus Risman remembered: At the 2015 Challenge Cup final, at Wembley, a memorial statue was unveiled to five rugby league legends. Gus Risman (top) holds the Cup. Martin Offiah, Alex Murphy, Doreen Ashton (wife of Eric), myself and Billy Boston commemorate a very special occasion.

Picture perfect: With a portrait of my father.

Three internationals: My brother John and I take pride in an image of our father at Mike Stephenson's rugby league museum, formerly at the George Hotel, Huddersfield.

Proud day: Receiving my OBE for Services to Rugby Union and Rugby League in 2011. Also pictured is Ann (with her OBE for Services to Further Education in 1999) and our sons Michael (Wellington College, Cambridge University, Rugby RUFC, England Colts, Rosslyn Park), *left*, Martin (Wellington College, Loughborough College, Camberley, Guildford and Godalming, Surrey) and John (Wellington College, Transvaal Under 19s, Oxford University, Richmond RUFC), *right*. John was the first player to win a double Varsity Blue for union and league.

campaign and the first part of the new 1966-67 season was eventful to say the least.

We played Hunslet in the traditional Lazenby Cup charity match, winning 28-10 but I tweaked a thigh muscle and was out injured before the season proper even started.

I missed a couple of matches, Syd Hynes played full-back in my absence and Mick Shoebottom scored a record 30 points in a win against Batley, including kicking nine goals.

I obviously needed to get fit again quickly and our winning run in the league continued as I returned to the team, including sweet revenge over Wigan in a thriller.

Off the field, Leeds had new floodlights installed to add to the revolutionary underground heating, making Headingley the finest club rugby ground in the country.

A new competition, the Mackeson trophy was introduced with awards for the top points scoring teams in the league which Leeds won in the first part of the season.

We met Bradford in a top of the table clash and came away with a convincing 27-7 victory cementing our place as leaders, for once I finally did get one over on Dad.

Our first defeat came to an end at St. Helens in a match where the four tackle rule was not in operation but we then went on another successful run, losing only two out of 15 matches and consolidating our position.

We had now established ourselves as the team to beat and had taken a stranglehold in the table with significant victories over Saints and Wigan.

Steady progress was maintained in the Challenge Cup with victories over Blackpool and Oldham.

Alan Smith best sums up the feeling in the camp at the time.

"We started to see the fulfilment of Roy's ambitions as a coach and trainer with the blend of youth in the back line and a pack, all of them, fitter and faster than they had ever been in their careers, able to run other teams ragged, particularly in the last 20 minutes.

"Bev at full-back must have marvelled at times, like I did out on the wing, at the spectacle of rugby being served up in front of him.

"The introduction of the four tackle rule played right in to Roy's hands. He had players standing so deep on attack that it pulled advancing defences about as the ball was moved rapidly travelling through the hands of players coming on to it at top speed.

"The perfect complement to this rampaging new team was having Bev at the back, with that assuring air of composure and positional sense which would deal with any type of player likely to break our defence.

"I never saw a winger or indeed any player go round him or through him."

My goal kicking had been going well and Cyril Kellett and I were embroiled in a battle to be leading exponent.

The press was speculating about which of us would get to 100 goals first before Christmas, I had never been anywhere near these targets before so it was new territory for me.

I've always been a great believer in statistics and records, particularly personal landmarks, so I was keen to win the battle.

He got there one match before me but I got my own back later finishing as leading marksman in the league with 163 goals for the season.

Leeds were the most prolific try scorers in my four full seasons so I probably had more opportunities than most but, regardless, I was proud to head the standings three times in succession and coming close to Lewis Jones's club records.

We ran away with the league leader's title, tying up the top spot before the end of March with another string of victories.

All the talk now was of making it a Championship and cup treble and the success-starved fans were dreaming of great things. Disastrously, we got ahead of ourselves and failed miserably in the Cup semi-final against underdogs Featherstone Rovers.

They were a tough, uncompromising side with a formidable pack of forwards including Les Tonks, Arnie Morgan and Jimmy Thompson and driven on by half-backs Tommy Smales and Carl Dooler.

They took us apart in the mud at Huddersfield.

We couldn't lift ourselves for the play offs despite a first round victory against Widnes, then meeting our on-form arch rivals Castleford in the next round with Hardisty, Hepworth and Hartley ruling the roost and lost at Headingley 13-9.

It was a dismal end to the season after promising so much, perhaps we were not quite ready but our mixture of hard-bitten veterans and rapidly improving youngsters was coming together and Mick Clark started to show what an outstanding prop forward he was as he took over the captaincy.

I was disappointed that we could not carry our form to the end of the season because my first full year had been by far my most successful.

I'd played consistently and more or less injury free, received the 'Player of the Year' award from the Leeds Supporters Club and shared the 'Best and Fairest' accolade given by the Referees Association, with Arthur Keegan.

There was no unbeaten start to the 1967-68 season as we lost early on to St Helens and were surprisingly beaten by

Batley 13-12 as injuries mounted. We lost Drew Broatch and then John Atkinson with a dislocated shoulder and improvisations were called for.

I played several matches at stand-off with Mick Shoebottom moved to scrum-half as we had no obvious replacement for the little general Barry Seabourne.

Despite that, we continued to win matches but unfortunately lost to Hull in the Yorkshire Cup final, our reserves had worked wonders but just couldn't stand up to the Airlie Birds at their aggressive best.

We also had two monumental battles against league front runners Bradford Northern which finished one win each.

Particularly memorable was the match at Headingley when we were treated to a goal kicking masterclass by their young Welsh rugby union prodigy, Terry Price who landed seven goals from all distances and angles.

Youngsters like Phil Sunderland, Pete Fozzard, Dave Hick, John Langley, Frank Brown and Chris Fawdington had all come through with flying colours and we had also tried to sign star players including Frank Foster and Bill Holliday, but Hull K.R. was having none of it and turned down our requests.

We had to battle on and started to turn things round as players returned from injury, particularly our playmakers Ray Batten and Barry Seaborne.

It was good to get closer to the action at stand-off although I must admit it got rather tough at times, I got a bit knocked about and it seemed as if everyone was firing at my head.

There was one particular incident when I had an altercation with Dave Horn the notorious Bramley prop forward.

We were having a torrid time against them when I got the ball with only big Dave in front of me.

He had quite a reputation and took every opportunity to annihilate his opponents whenever possible.

I fancied my chances to try out my side step, Dave stood his ground as I approached and I tripped over and fell head first towards him.

He couldn't believe his luck as my unprotected head dropped directly in the way of his closed fist and he didn't hesitate and gave me a beautiful uppercut straight to the forehead which opened up like a ripe tomato with blood flying all over the place.

Needless to say I was carried off to be stitched up although, surprisingly, Dave stayed on, the referee saw nothing wrong because I had fallen into the tackle.

I did come back on, stitches and all, and scored a try, so honours even.

I returned to full-back and had eyes on a Test place again as the Kangaroos arrived and once more my name came up on the list of likely candidates for selection.

My old friend Arthur Keegan was holding down the full-back spot and got the nod and the nearest I came to selection was a run out in a RL XIII against the tourists.

I couldn't grumble at their choice because Arthur was a fabulous player, courageous, talented a good goal kicker and one of the best defensive last lines in the game.

Australia proved just too strong yet again and clinched a highly entertaining series two-one despite the absence of their captain the great Reg Gasnier.

More or less at the same time, Dad decided to come out of retirement at the age of 55 and played in a veteran's team alongside his long-time friend and colleague fellow Welshman Trevor Foster in a charity match at Headingley.

It was wonderful to see him out there again mesmerising one and all.

In contrast to our previous campaign, when we dominated the league virtually from start to finish, we hung in this time and gradually got back to full strength, significantly, we also signed Bill Ramsey who bolstered our pack just when it was needed.

We embarked on a record-equalling 18-match unbeaten run, with the spectators treated to some vintage rugby.

At international level, Great Britain had been struggling having won only two out of the previous six matches, our status had fallen considerably and even France were proving difficult.

After the series setback against Australia, the third on the trot, the selectors lost patience and wielded the axe, making seven changes for the match in Paris in the New Year.

There were promises of a whole new approach to the preparation with regular training sessions and practice matches against club opposition, it was a revolution and excellent long term planning for the World Cup in Australia in June 1968.

My form had been good but I was just enjoying the ride with Leeds when the squad was announced with five new caps; Mick Clark, Ray French, Arnie Morgan, Derek Edwards and me – I was absolutely thrilled when I heard the news of my selection – I was to be a dual-international.

Yet again, Ray French and I had followed the same path winning our first caps together after years of waiting.

The home and away matches were to be played in February and March and a comprehensive build up was planned with training sessions and matches against Salford.

The squad was given every opportunity under coach

Colin Hutton and captain Neil Fox and we were full of confidence prior to the opening clash at Parc des Princes.

Everything worked to perfection for both me and the team as we overpowered a strong French side in a superb first half performance.

I was revelling in the chance to show what I could do at international level and with the pack dominating and Tommy Bishop and Roger Millward weaving their magic, I had the freedom of the park running the ball out of defence and supporting breaks to finish with two tries.

My goal kicking was on song too and I finished with a tally of 16 points in our 22-13 victory.

The return match at Odsal was like something after the Lord Mayor's show.

The 13,000 crowd were expecting a feast of running rugby after our convincing victory but the French were no pushovers, scored an early try and with a flurry of high tackles and the usual incomprehensible refereeing by a French whistler, we never really got into our stride and had to make do with occasional flashes of brilliance.

Our speedy backs Alan Burwell, Chris Young and Roger Millward led us to a 19-8 victory which was satisfactory but we were left with a feeling of unfinished business.

I was reasonably pleased with my second Great Britain performance apart from poor goal kicking and we all realised that there was much work to be done if we were going to be able to compete at the World Cup.

The domestic season now reached its peak.

In the Challenge Cup Leeds had not done themselves justice since last being at Wembley in 1957, but we gave ourselves every chance again in 1968.

An unconvincing victory against a stubborn

Liverpool City in the first round at Headingley was followed by a demolition job in our home tie against Bramley.

A tough encounter with Oldham at their notorious Watersheddings ground saw us squeeze through 13-0 to set up our third semi-final in three years, against nemesis Wigan.

Our chequered history at this stage weighed heavily on our minds but we were right at the peak of our powers and were increasingly confident that this was our year.

It was a beautiful day, the Station Road ground at Swinton was in perfect condition and this time we made no mistake putting illustrious Wigan to the sword with the best Leeds performance for many a year.

The fans were delirious as our exciting young backs ran riot with tries by John Atkinson, Bernard Watson, Syd Hynes and Barry Seaborne.

John's try was one of the best ever scored in such a game, he left Billy Boston for dead and majestically rounded Colin Tyrer on a 60 yard run to touch the ball down near the posts.

Our mobile forwards took the Wigan pack apart with Bill Ramsey at his very best and scoring a brilliant try.

I tacked on five goals while I watched the exceptional show unfold from the back, it was the epitome of the Francis way and we had made it to Wembley at last.

We clinched the league leader's trophy and prepared for the Championship play-offs in the lead up to the Cup final.

I picked up a slight back injury and didn't play in the opening match against Widnes nor the next round when Wigan again got the upper hand at Headingley.

That was disappointing but now, at last, we were able to concentrate on Wembley.

Watersplash, World Cup and Champions

11

Leeds seemed to get to Wembley about every ten years so the fans were at fever pitch in the run up to the '68 final.

Our opponents were Wakefield, captained by Harold Poynter, and Trinity were in prime form having clinched the Championship for the second year in succession the week before, they were on for the double.

A titanic struggle was forecast between the best teams over previous two seasons, on the grandest stage with Wakefield the slight favourites, having had the experience of winning at Wembley three times already in the decade.

The match promised to be a classic and it was, perhaps the most enthralling final ever in the sport, but no one anticipated just what sort of mesmerising drama it would turn out to be.

We were at full strength but Wakefield suffered a severe blow when Neil Fox, their talisman, who had been suffering a troublesome groin injury for a number of weeks, failed to make their starting line-up. Significantly for me, he was also forced to withdraw from the World Cup squad due to leave for the Antipodes straight after the Final.

The national stadium in mid-May was expected to be a shirt-sleeved occasion but heavy rain in the days before the match had left water on the pitch.

Although game day dawned sunny and sultry, the travelling hordes from West Yorkshire were suddenly caught in a spectacular thunderstorm, engulfed in a torrential downpour, as they made their way down Wembley Way and towards the twin towers, behind which the beautiful green turf was becoming submerged.

Although the rain stopped well before kick-off, large areas of the pitch were still covered in puddles and as we went out for the routine walkabout to gauge the atmosphere in our best club suits, the water was coming up over our shoes.

Even with that distraction, it was still an unforgettable moment to walk on the hallowed ground and listen to the roars of our supporters as they started to fill the stadium.

The conditions were so bad that several from the governing body, BBC and stadium officials were starting to question whether the match could go ahead.

The decision had to be left to the referee, Mr. John Hebblethwaite from York who had a king-size dilemma as start time approached.

Under normal circumstances, the surface would have been judged unplayable, however he decided that the pitch was not sufficiently dangerous and because the bulk of the near-capacity crowd were either at or in the stadium, the game should go ahead.

Foolhardy or courageous, the decision led to one of the most talked about matches of all time.

Ironically, as we emerged from the tunnel to a gigantic roar on the long walk to the centre circle, the sun shone through the ominous black clouds.

We had received our pep talk from Roy Francis who wanted us to put on a show on par with the semi-final display against Wigan, but little did we realise how the conditions would affect that.

We tried to remain focussed as our boots disappeared below water level as we lined up for the opening ceremony and anthems.

Nevertheless, I thought I was walking on air experiencing a feeling of total exhilaration to be involved in a Challenge Cup final, an occasion that had been such a part of our lives growing up when Dad had been involved.

What followed next was a mixture of drama, comedy and even farce in this magnificent theatre, agonies and ecstasies for all involved with the result in the balance to the very last second.

The pitch was a cross between a skating rink and a lake, one minute the players were gliding across it, next skidding and falling or wallowing in great pools of water like a herd of hippos.

Many of those watching live or on national television claimed the match was reduced to a lottery, with the teams of the season and their outstanding players blunted in the most atrocious conditions.

Yet despite the numerous handling errors created by the large piece of soap masquerading as a ball, the crowd was treated to a duel of physical endeavour and no little skill.

The forwards battered each other to a standstill with our skipper Mick Clark, the Eyre brothers Albert and Ken, and Bill Ramsey responding to the promptings of Ray Batten and our little admiral Barry Seabourne.

In response, David Jeanes, Bob Haigh and Matt McLeod did likewise as Poynton and Neil's brother Don Fox tried to rule the roost.

Leeds hooker Tony Crosby got the better of George Shepherd although, as he said afterwards in the communal bath, he almost drowned in the scrums as his head sank into the puddles time and again.

Possession was a dubious advantage as ball handling was more of a hazard and the emphasis had to be on causing the opposition to make mistakes near their own line.

Don tried to put us under pressure with long raking kicks away from me where the ball either skidded or stuck in the water.

Our little maestro Barry went through his full repertoire of pinpoint chip-kicks, grubbers and punts to retaliate in style.

I spent most my time cleaning up Fox's kicks, concentrating so that I did not make mistakes and running the ball back whenever possible.

Despite Poynton and Mick Shoebottom revelling in the conditions regardless, as the first half progressed it was something of a stalemate.

Early on I got a chance with a penalty and took my time even more than usual to make sure that I made no mistake.

It was a great feeling as the ball floated between the posts to notch the first points of the match. Don Fox and I then exchanged a penalty each to make the score 4-2 to Leeds.

The result ultimately hinged on a series of totally unpredictable incidents caused by human error due to the extreme weather conditions.

After about 20 minutes, Don drove yet another cross field kick away from me towards our left corner.

As the ball skidded along, John Atkinson hurtled back and just stopped it from going into touch but as he turned he lost his footing and slid helplessly into the greyhound track barriers.

He had set the ball up perfectly for Ken Hurst, the Wakefield winger, to hack on with no one else in sight and touch down for a try, Don converted and we were 7-4 behind.

We battled away until just before half time, the storm clouds gathering again and as if to recognise their part in the unfolding drama they released another torrent of rain.

The crowd was stunned, some ran for cover as the lightening flashed overhead, thunder cracked and a torrential downpour soaked players and spectators alike.

It flooded the pitch once again as we sought the sanctuary of the changing room.

Tactics were clear for both sides in the second half, keep the opposition going backwards with more tactical kicking.

It wasn't what we'd planned, we wanted to run them ragged but instead Fox and Seabourne produced a stirring, engrossing kicking duel.

Defences held but were stretched to the limit until late in the second half when yet another kick through by Barry was chased by John Atkinson, he got to the ball marginally before the Wakefield defenders, hacked on once and then again to the try line.

Despairing dives by half the Wakefield team failed to secure the ball and an arm was held out which partially impeded John's progress as the ball crossed the try line.

Sensationally, referee Hebblethwaite was signalling for a penalty try as Ian Brooke, the Trinity centre came away with the ball.

Wakefield and their fans were completely stunned as

I converted from in front of the posts to put us 9-7 ahead, while we could sense the ecstasy of victory.

To this day the arguments still rage as to the legitimacy of that decision.

If you want a comprehensive analysis of this incident and, indeed the whole event, you should read *They Walked on Water* by former MP David Hinchliffe, in which he explores every nuance to underline the injustice that he believes Wakefield suffered.

Despite that, we are still very good friends.

As he says: "When Bev and Ann get their annual Christmas card from the 'Return the 1968 Medals Campaign, Holmfirth Branch' they know exactly who it has come from.

"Like many Wakefield Trinity supporters of my generation I have held a life-long belief that Leeds were gifted the Challenge Cup that year because of the highly questionable awarding of an obstruction try. But whatever the subjective opinions of rival fans on the outcome, the 'Watersplash' final was arguably rugby league's most famous, with the incredible drama lasting until its final seconds.

"And the record shows that it was the boot of Bev Risman – in frankly impossible conditions – that was the difference between the sides."

There was still time for Wakefield to rescue the situation and the next few minutes are forever imprinted on my memory because I suddenly became a major player in the saga.

With time running out and Wakefield pinned in their own half, the referee awarded a penalty for a scrum offence.

It was virtually full-time and we had to decide whether I should go for goal and run down the clock or kick for touch and keep the ball near the Wakefield line until the whistle went.

We had a word with the referee about how long there was still to go and he implied that time was more or less up so we presumed that this would be the last kick.

Skipper Mick Clark decided that I should take the shot at goal provided I could get the ball over the dead-ball line so we would it back from the restart as insurance.

Deliberating and eating up the seconds, I concentrated on making solid contact in order to, at least, get the distance and I struck it perfectly, surprising myself a little as the ball sailed over the bar to put us two more points ahead.

Surely that was it, we actually thought it was all over and were still celebrating when Mr Hebblethwaite decided to give Wakefield one more chance by allowing them a last restart.

The referee was in sole charge of the timekeeping in those days but still we only had to gather the ball from the kick off and the silverware was ours.

But Don Fox surprised us by kicking the ball along the ground away from his forwards, it went straight towards Bernard Watson our centre but he couldn't gather it as Ken Hirst came racing up and kicked the ball past him towards the posts.

Leeds players all over the pitch stood mesmerised as I tried to turn and cover but Hirst shot past me as the ball came to rest in the in-goal area. He triumphantly splashed on top of it for a try that narrowed the gap to a point with the winning conversion, surely, to come.

I had my head in my hands in abject horror, we had gone from pent-up elation to absolute despair.

We trudged back behind the try line, most unable to look as Don Fox stepped up to steal our glory, I was heartbroken, livid and in denial.

Don had kicked brilliantly all through the match but no one will ever truly know his state of mind at that moment and the enormous pressure he was under to deliver Trinity the double for the first time in their history.

In disbelief, I stared as he hardly got the ball off the ground and screwed it to the right of the posts, sinking to his knees distraught.

The incident is now part of sporting folklore as one of the greatest errors of all time and my emotions were in absolute turmoil.

I went from joy to desolation back to thrilled, not knowing whether to laugh or cry as I jumped up as the whistle blew and we'd done it.

There was a momentary hush and then the place erupted as it dawned on the Leeds fans that we had actually won and hopes and dreams had been fulfilled in the most extraordinary circumstances.

My brain was in a whirl as we danced and hugged. A hollow victory? Not for me, I'd won at Wembley. Sympathy for Don? Certainly.

I had a lingering concern too, Ann watching the desperate drama unfold in the grandstand was two weeks overdue with our third son Michael.

She'd insisted on going to Wembley regardless and travelled with a chaperone, her friend Joyce, and our doctor and I had visions that the sheer excitement would have induced her. All I could think of was whether she was okay, but when I finally picked her out she was dancing away with all the rest.

When I reflect on my years in rugby, it strikes me that most of the memorable matches I played in were under extreme weather conditions which had some significance in determining the result.

I was no stranger to mud, wind and water growing up in Cumberland, one of the wettest places in England.

Our school pitch was little more than a ploughed field most of the time and for my school's international debut in the supposedly idyllic South of France, we arrived in a monsoon and the match had to be postponed for a day.

When we eventually did take the field it, was covered in pools of water and we drew nil-nil, and the thick mud at Cardiff Arms Park in my first rugby union international caused my disallowed try.

Wembley over, we had no real time to take in the win as there was the need to get ready for the World Cup in Australia and New Zealand .

All those who had played in the Tests against the French were re-selected along with Mick Shoebottom (Leeds), Clive Sullivan (Hull), Kevin Ashcroft (Leigh) and Bob Haigh (Wakefield).

There was, however, one significant omission.

Neil Fox, who had captained the team against France failed to overcome his groin injury and had to withdraw, a serious blow to our chances of success.

John Atkinson was chosen as Neil's replacement and I was surprised and immensely honoured to be selected as the new tour skipper.

It was a wonderful feeling to emulate my father who had captained the Great Britain Lions in 1946.

Before getting down to the logistics and mechanics of the trip, Leeds and Wakefield had to deal with the aftermath of the extraordinary events of the cup final.

Controversy reverberated around the rugby league world, not least about whether the game should have been allowed to go ahead.

We enjoyed our celebrations, starting at the Park Lane

Hotel in London on Saturday evening and continuing with a parade around Leeds and the Mayor's reception.

The only one who seemed unhappy by what had happened was Roy Francis who felt his team had been denied the chance to show what it was truly capable of.

Wakefield could not accept their defeat and Mick Clark, our captain and in the World Cup party but with our roles reversed, was moved to say that the match was a lottery and neither side deserved to lose.

Immediately following the Wembley weekend, the tour party gathered in Leeds for the final countdown.

We had already met on a number of occasions and this group was better prepared than any previous national side leaving the shores.

The last week included the fitting of our official uniforms, photographs and media interviews, we had a practice match against Leeds and a couple of training sessions prior to our departure, no stone had been left unturned by our management team of coach Colin Hutton, Bill Fallowfield the manager and RFL chairman John Smallwood.

I still had one major problem, our third child. There was still no sign of the arrival and Ann and I had to accept that the birth would not happen before I left for Australia.

She was determined that I should go and just as when she went to Wembley we tried to cover all eventualities.

There must have been a miscalculation somewhere because it was another ten days before Michael was born at five o'clock in the morning prior to our game against New Zealand.

I was awoken in my hotel bedroom to take a call from Bradford to receive the wonderful news personally from Ann who had managed to persuade the staff at the Infirmary to let her use the telephone.

They were very good natured about it but shocked to find out that she was actually ringing half way around the world from the delivery room to give me the news.

Great Britain had been established as second favourites for the tournament, 16 years after last winning it and when we arrived in Sydney the media circus was there lying in wait for us.

Excitement was at fever pitch leading up to our opening match against favourites Australia a few days later.

The schedule was very tight but unavoidable due to the late finish of our season and we now had to overcome the considerable effects of jet lag and get in as much training as possible in the build up to the match.

It would have been so much better if we could have arrived a week or so earlier, get acclimatised and play one or two warm up games.

Instead we played our warm up matches after the World Cup finished on a pioneering four match tour of Queensland!

There was no doubt in my mind that the very short preparation time was one of the reasons for our poor performance in the opener.

Perhaps it was a ploy to undermine us, along with the wonderful hospitality and the seemingly endless media and other events that we had to attend.

As captain, I was much in demand to give my opinion on a host of often irrelevant topics, even to the extent of having to give views on my taste in women.

Training had to be fitted into the schedule and in no time at all we were in the changing room getting ready to do battle in front of a capacity crowd of over 60,000 at the Sydney Cricket Ground.

It was a critical match to start with because whoever

won would be firm favourites to go through to the final. The losers would still have an opportunity by winning both of their remaining matches against France and New Zealand in the round robin format.

We reckoned that we were in with a good chance as Australia were in a transition stage and our successful build up against the French had given us plenty of confidence.

Before kick-off, John Percival the New Zealand referee came into the changing room and proceeded to lecture us about the rules.

He told us quite firmly what he would and wouldn't allow, warning us about a host of sanctionable offences, as captain I took his instructions on board.

Then came one of my proudest-ever moments, leading Great Britain out onto the famous Sydney cricket ground as my father had done many years before.

Mr Percival, however, proceeded to ruin the match, penalising us from the off for a series of apparent offences which even the usually one-eyed Aussie media failed to see.

In the end we were at a loss as to how to deal the barrage of penalties particularly at the scrum as Kevin Ashcroft, our fiery hooker, came in for particular attention and showed some dissent for which he was penalised again.

Eric Sims, the green and gold's debutant full-back had the easiest of introductions as he landed two early, settling penalties before we could get into the game.

We did come back, though, and briefly went into the lead when some Tommy Bishop magic put Ian Brooke over for a try and I converted.

It didn't last as Sims kicked three more goals to put the hosts into a lead they never lost. We were somewhat demoralised, eventually losing the penalty count 18-7 and the match 25-10.

Although Australia won convincingly in the end, it left a very bad taste and was a controversial start to our tour.

My mind went back to the British Lions Rugby Union Test in 1959, in Dunedin, when we were similarly baulked by Kiwi referee.

Percival was pilloried by the media and called upon to justify his actions.

He said that every penalty was for a legitimate offence and the cause was Great Britain's regular infringing of the rules and lack of discipline, and that was that.

We had got off to a terrible start and as skipper I felt a greater responsibility for us to qualify for the final.

I've never quite understood why our next match against France was in New Zealand and our final game back in Australia against the Kiwis.

We found ourselves off to Auckland to prepare for the must-win game at Carlaw Park which necessitated complicated and time wasting arrangements that did not help our preparations.

The weather, typical of the land of the long white cloud, was unpredictable and Carlaw Park notorious for the abysmal state of the pitch whenever there was rain.

It came down in bucket loads and the grass instead was a sea of mud and water beforehand, that shouldn't have been an issue for us but it was a leveller.

The surface became almost unplayable as more rain came down as the match progressed.

Starting with the two matches against France in February and March our new strategy had been to play to the strengths of our half-backs, Tommy Bishop and Roger Millward and our speedy three-quarters.

The weather and ground conditions worked against us on the day as France resorted to rugged defence and a tactical kicking game, not their usual tactics. We got bogged down in the mud as they kept pressure on defensively and the contest developed into an arm-wrestle.

They adapted to the conditions much better and we found it more and more difficult to get out of the mire.

At two-all with ten minutes or so to go, it looked as though we were heading for stalemate and all on the last round of games, when yet another kick through by France at last produced something out of nothing and they scrambled over for a try and they hung on for a famous victory.

We were out of the World Cup!

It was a monumental disaster and the worst moment in my rugby league life, the team was devastated, we had gone to pieces at the critical moment.

Great credit to France, they had produced the shock of the tournament but no-one could see them defeating Australia in the final and the whole event was effectively over as a spectacle.

After all our efforts, all we could look forward to was our wooden spoon contest against New Zealand in Sydney.

The spirit in the camp was low as we slunk back to Australia but we gathered ourselves together determined to go out at least with all guns blazing in an attempt to regain some of our pride.

We did have the satisfaction of a comfortable victory in front of a paltry 15,000 fans who were lost inside the SCG, winning 38-14 and in the process broke a number of records, my seven goals were the most by a British player.

All that after being woken up at five o'clock on the morning of the match to learn of Michael's safe arrival, at least my World Cup experience had a happy ending and I couldn't wait to get back to hold him.

I was ready for home but our trip was not over yet as

we set off on a pioneering trip around the Northern areas of Queensland where we won all four games, playing in glorious weather on bone hard pitches and running up 119 points.

We entertained enthusiastic crowds with the sort of rugby we would have liked to have provided in the tournament and enjoyed the relaxation and wonderful hospitality which, to a certain extent, helped to soften the blow of our desperately disappointing campaign.

On returning home, I couldn't wait to get out onto Baildon Moor behind our house with my livewire sons as they tried to catch a few rabbits with the boomerangs I had brought them.

The 1968-69 season was fast approaching and with two consecutive league leaders' trophies and a Challenge Cup victory, we had established ourselves as the outstanding team in.

Pre-season training was in full flow and the opening fixtures were eagerly awaited. All the players involved in the World Cup couldn't wait to put it behind them, me especially, having been the leader.

At Headingley, there was still empty space in the trophy cabinet because we had yet to win the Yorkshire Cup as a group and were still searching for the ultimate success, the Championship, which somewhat bizarrely given its standing, the club had only ever won once, eight years before.

I felt that the team would be even stronger with more of our local talent coming through; Frank Brown, John Burke, Trevor Briggs, Pete Fozzard, Chris Fawdington, Phil Holmes, Phil Cookson and Graham Eccles would all be blooded during the season.

Ron Cowan and Drew Broatch were returning from long term injuries and we had also signed speedster Mike

Lamb from Headingley rugby union. Barry Seaborne, Ray Batten and Mick Shoebottom were in their pomp along with our star wingers John Atkinson and Alan Smith, and Syd Hynes and Bernard Watson were joined by John Langley to give us great strength in midfield.

A new name appeared on the horizon too, at full-back, as 16 year old John Holmes made his bow in a career which would see him become one of the all-time greats, I knew I would have to watch my step.

Our forwards were revelling in the Roy Francis regime of fast-flowing rugby, we had tasted success and were thirsty for another big season.

But we were in for an early season shock as the news came through that Roy would be leaving for pastures new in Australia just when he was at the peak of his powers.

As we pondered who might take over, we won the traditional pre-season, charity Lazenby Cup match with neighbours Hunslet, with the precocious John Holmes playing in my absence and kicking 10 goals and claiming 26 points on debut.

We were ready for the first match away to Alex Murphy-led Leigh and shock number two, they beat us 22-19 and after all our high expectations we were well and truly brought down to earth.

It wasn't the way we wanted to send Roy off and we immediately went on a 12 match undefeated run including away victories over Hull, Featherstone and Halifax in the Yorkshire Cup taking us to the final against Castleford.

That was the first of five bitter duels against our arch rivals, we had our full strength, 'watersplash' side out against an intimidating Cas pack including Ron Hill, Brian Lockwood and Malcolm Reilly and led by mercurial stand-off Alan Hardisty, and they fancied their chances.

It was a glorious day and perfect conditions at Wakefield's Belle Vue, tailor made for a classic in front of a capacity crowd who were not disappointed.

Fortunes fluctuated in a terrific contest and in a desperate finish we clinched the match with a try by substitute Dave Hick which I converted, taking my goal tally to five as we ran out 22-11 winners.

We went from strength to strength and finished top of the table for the third year in succession, losing only three matches despite some desperate upheaval.

Roy departed to take up his new role with North Sydney as Christmas approached and we were then hit by the sudden tragic death of Jack Nelson, our 'A' team coach who had only just taken over the reins.

Joe Warham stepped into the breach and steered the club through the end of the season, Barry Seaborne taking over as captain when Mick Clark decided to step down.

Disruption or not, we kept winning and I was having a golden spell with goal kicking, landing 99 up to Christmas and then finishing the season with 165, my best-ever tally and only one short of Lewis Jones's record.

It included a 12-goal personal record in our 63-11 win against Batley and a short barren spell when I went off the boil for a couple of matches and one dreadful occasion when I kicked only one out of six at Halifax.

I had a major mishap there too when I was concussed and stretchered off only to wake up and find Ann standing over me in the changing room.

Apparently I had been wandering aimlessly around the pitch unattended and, fearful of a serious injury, she had run onto the pitch in the middle of the play waving her umbrella to attract the referee's attention and then stayed with me as I was carried off.

Our winning streak extended to 17 games until we finally lost to Bradford Northern in the final fixture.

Whilst the league offered many highs, there was a low in the third round of the Cup against Castleford.

We were defending our trophy and having beaten them three times already that season, were favourites going to Wheldon Road in front of their fervent supporters.

There were a few scores to settle from the previous matches and the occasion turned nasty as Cas tried to rough us up, with Barry Seaborne coming in for some special treatment.

We failed to deal with the situation and their overly aggressive approach paid dividends for once as they beat us 9-5 in an ugly match.

By now, despite having avoided serious injury, I was beginning to wonder how much longer I could continue playing at this level as I was approaching 32 years old.

The demands of my teaching job were increasing and in order to maintain my fitness, I had to step up my training programme.

I hadn't shared these concerns with anyone but I was beginning to consider retirement, possibly at the end of the season.

The dilemma was that I was playing as well as I ever had and the team was on the crest of a wave.

The previous November there had been one of the annual fixtures against France and the guys who had played in the World Cup were keen to repair the damage.

But that squad was decimated and nine newcomers were brought in, I was one of the casualties despite playing better than ever for my club.

Neil Fox was brought back and Arthur Keegan preferred to me at full-back and I couldn't even get in to either the Welsh or the English teams for the domestic internationals.

The selectors had obviously decided to make yet another fresh start and abandoned their previous policies.

I was extremely disappointed to miss out and had no grumbles with Arthur's selection but the most remarkable thing, though, was that despite Leeds's many successes, we had no player in the Great Britain team.

I was very proud of my short but eventful International career in league but I accepted that it was now all over bar a miracle with no more fixtures on the immediate horizon.

Domestically, we finished the season in style firmly implanted in first place and also pocketing the Yorkshire League trophy.

With no other distractions, we were able to give our full attention to the Championship play-offs where we had previously tailed off and disappointed in the seasons when we had been the most consistent side in the league.

We were guaranteed home matches and disposed of Oldham in the first round, 32-12, and had a really tough battle with Workington's rugged pack to get through the next when I posted one of our four tries.

We met a star studded Salford in the semi-final who fielded David Watkins, Bill Burgess, Chris Hesketh, Mike Coulman and Colin Dixon but triumphed 22-12 in a spectacular match, with restored Ronnie Cowan superb scoring two tries as we breezed into the final.

Our opponents were, needless to say, Castleford who were looking to complete the double having won at Wembley.

There had been no love lost between us in the four previous meetings during the season and there was much posturing between the clubs in the build-up.

But no one anticipated the mayhem that occurred in the match both on the field and the terraces as players and supporters alike gave vent to their feelings.

It created an explosive atmosphere and an unusual need for police intervention to stop fighting amongst the fans.

There had been doubts about the fitness of our skipper Barry Seaborne as his long-standing dislocated shoulder came out again in the semi.

He courageously pleaded that he was fit to play in the decider when he patently wasn't, but he was an important cog in our wheel so it was decided that we would take the chance.

I have never played in a match of such brutality as incident upon incident had to be dealt with by referee Billy Thompson who, despite his reputation as a disciplinarian, was unable to keep the sides in check.

Scores had to be settled and forwards on both sides were constantly involved in acts of thuggery, particularly as the score remained close well into the second half.

Between the fighting, there were glimpses of the outstanding play for which both sides were famous but it was generally overshadowed by the constant foul play.

I'd kicked two goals in the first half but we were 11-7 down at the break and the dressing room at the interval looked like a triage post.

There was blood and bandages everywhere, our skipper Mick Clark had his head taped up but was soon after withdrawn from the fray and Barry finally succumbed to his shoulder, which had to be put back in a number of times.

Cas suffered similar misfortune, losing Malcolm Reilly and Keith Hepworth and, in between the mayhem, I landed another penalty.

I was spending most of the time fielding a variety of

kicks and trying to run the ball back into what appeared to be a brick wall.

I became more and more spattered with mud and blood and engulfed by the Castleford heavy brigade and frequently belted in the face for my sins.

Then, out of the blue, the match turned into a classic.

In typical poaching fashion Alan Hardisty ghosted onto a long stray pass from Mick Joyce and cantered clear, it was his party piece and he'd been waiting nearly all the game for the chance.

I chased back desperately the 40 yards with no chance of catching him but managed to steer him towards the touch line and away from the posts, far enough to make the conversion too difficult for Mick Redfern.

Five points down going in to the closing stages, we were struggling but Mick Shoebottom made a superb break to bring us close to the Castleford line and Bill Ramsey promptly popped over a drop goal.

I wasn't sure it was the right decision feeling, perhaps, that we should have gone for a try in order to equalise.

Almost on full-time we had one more throw of the dice, Redfern kicked long and deep into our territory, an awkward bounce saw the Castleford chasers overrun the ball and it fell into our hands.

Two wide passes and it reached me around our 25 yard line with their defence seemingly in disarray, I skirted around a couple of exhausted forwards and suddenly the whole field opened up in front of me.

The try line looked miles away, I made ground but with the defenders frantically trying to cut me off there was no way that I was going to make it with half the field still to go.

I had no support but then saw John Atkinson hurtling

up the left touchline but too far away for a pass but the try line was completely open so I left footed the ball into space and in front of him.

He judged the bounce perfectly, took the ball in his stride, outpaced the cover and triumphantly planted the ball down to the left of the posts – we were level!

I had the conversion to win the match and tried to keep my composure as I prepared for the most important kick of my life, concentrating on my technique.

I had to clear my mind and it wasn't Don Fox's notorious miss against us at Wembley that was worrying me but that we had a family holiday booked on the Monday and I desperately didn't want a replay.

It was not my cleanest strike but it went over, we had secured the sweetest of victories over our deadly rivals and we were the champions at last.

To crown everything, I won the Harry Sunderland trophy as man of the match.

Alan Smith recalls: "Alan Hardisty intercepted, he was away down centre field in a flash.

"Bev facing the wrong way, coming into attack, turned round and pushed him out towards the corner flag to limit the damage. Another few yards and he would have caught him.

"Then there was his collection of a high ball near the end of the game, with Leeds running out of time, against a charging, destructive Castleford pack.

"He beat the first man, swerved past two more and then placed the most accurate kick up field for my mate Atky to sprint over by the posts, job done.

"On attack, his timing coming into the line and the side step to split defences was a delight for the supporting players around him.

"Cool, unflappable, as in his training, he appeared to have another gear."

Whilst for jubilant coach Joe Warham: "The pattern was set early on with Dennis Hartley's robust assault on Bill Ramsey and, for Bev, it became an act of personal courage almost to field one of the many high kicks with vengeful opposing forwards bearing down.

"Here he proved to be one of the bravest, oozing his way through the opposition's ranks and for the winning try, his fine rugby brain engaged itself and almost instinctively the situation was appraised with the sweetest of punts ahead.

"A difficult and so critical match-winning conversion needed. No trouble! Not to one of the imperious Rismans."

Controversy raged afterwards and much was written and said about the animosity generated between us and how two clubs renowned for their wonderful rugby skills could produce such a disgraceful exhibition of near-continuous over-aggression.

But so much had been at stake, the occasion had become too much for both players and coaches.

Time is a great healer, though, and a few weeks later Derek Turner, arguably one the toughest players and coaches ever, left his job at Castleford to take over at Leeds.

The End of the Road

12

Lingering thoughts of retirement, not a bit of it, we had just completed our most successful season and had filled the cabinet with every trophy that it was possible to win.

The city of Leeds was celebrating the performances of its three major clubs, in one year, Leeds United, Yorkshire cricket and we at the Loiners had all won their respective championships and the City Council held a civic reception to celebrate the unique occasion.

It was great to rub shoulders with heroes such as Brian Close, Fred Trueman, Ray Illingworth, Jimmy Binks, Kevin Sharp and Geoff Cope, famous names from the pitch adjacent to us, alongside Billy Bremner, Norman Hunter, Jackie Charlton, Paul Madeley, Terry Cooper, Peter Lorimer, Johnny Giles and Gary Sprake, all household names in football.

Both teaching at Bradford, where my ambitions to eventually go into higher education had been fired, and rugby with Leeds had gone better than I could have imagined, I was probably at my fittest as the 1969-70 season approached.

Leeds were entering a new regime with 'Rocky' Turner taking over from my mentors Roy Francis and Joe Warham. It looked as if the gentle persuaders were being replaced by the iron fist and I wasn't quite sure what the immediate future held there.

The solution came from a most unexpected quarter, a new one year, full-time course leading to a masters degree in PE and sport, the first of its kind in the country, was being offered at Leeds University, exactly what I needed for my future career path outside the game and on my doorstep.

As a student, I would have more leisure time to devote to my rugby although the downside was that I would have to temporarily give up my teaching job, a decision which carried its own risks.

Kenneth Robinson, my understanding headmaster at BGS, proposed that I should take a year's secondment and the school would pay my salary if I returned after my studies.

It was a really tempting offer which I very much appreciated and though I'd really enjoyed my time there, I felt it was time to move on and take my chances.

Leeds were keen for me to continue and I really fancied the combination although, financially, we would need to keep winning – I had a family to support.

So it was agreed that I would play as required, there would be no guarantees and, of course, I had the precocious John Holmes waiting in the wings.

The plan was that we would share the full-back duties, I was prepared to help in any way I could and to give John as much help and advice as possible in order to establish him in the squad.

'Rocky' Turner was sceptical at first but as I continued to play well, I found myself selected on a regular basis although we both knew this was only a temporary measure.

He had inherited a highly successful side and wanted to put his own mark on the team and Mick Clark and I knew that we were not part of his long-term plans.

We were knocked out of the Yorkshire Cup at Hull in the semi-final and John and I shared the matches in an 11-week unbeaten spell but there was some unrest behind the scenes from those players who couldn't adjust to Rocky's abrasive style, some of whom left.

Nevertheless, we kept on winning and I played more frequently while he was signing some younger players and John found his feet in the 'A' team, proving to be an able deputy whenever he was called on to play.

I continued to maintain my form, was still knocking over the goals and really savouring my last season.

I was beginning to think I was indestructible when disaster struck.

We were playing Warrington at Wilderspool in the second round of the Challenge Cup on a grisly February afternoon with conditions treacherous underfoot.

The match was tight as we edged into an 8-5 lead when I joined the line and a break looked on as I tried to side step on the greasy surface.

My right leg buckled under me as my foot got stuck in the mud and I felt an excruciating pain in my knee.

I was helped off the field and I limped along the touchline, Eric Lewis our physio examined the injury and said that it didn't look good.

I pondered on the seriousness of it, wondering if the damage was to cartilage, ligaments or both.

It was the first time that I'd ever had anything wrong

with my right knee which had supported the dodgy left knee one for over a decade.

It was said that I only used my left leg for kicking goals and my right one for everything else, no wonder it finally gave way.

Fortunately, there was no major problem and I recovered quickly enough to be in contention for the game in the next round at Hull K.R. in early March.

We had our last training session on the main pitch at Headingley under the floodlights and the knee seemed okay as we finished off with a conditioned game of touch and pass.

John Atkinson broke away down the left and I thought I'd give the joint one last test and began to chase back.

I was sprinting freely, shadowing him down the wing and started to slow down as I ran over the touchline.

Suddenly I was on the floor in agony, my right leg had crumpled under me as I tripped on the step onto the surrounds.

This time I knew it was it was really serious as I was carried off to the changing room and without anyone telling me that my career would probably be over.

Even if I'd had an immediate operation, I would still be out for several weeks and with only ten left in the season, that was it.

The years of wear and tear had finally caught up, it looked like being a long process of rehabilitation and, in my heart I knew it was the end of professional rugby for me.

Psychologically I'd already got it in the back of mind that my career was coming to an end but the way it happened was devastating. I couldn't possibly be bitter after all I'd achieved but not going out on your own terms is something that haunts all sportspeople.

Alan Smith was a witness. "I feel sure we both share the same memories of those wonderful years at Leeds, the team spirit both on and off the pitch was tremendous," he recalls.

"Bev's decision to call time on his playing days, I thought, came a little early, but at 33 and with a young John Holmes being groomed to take over the position, he had already worked out there was life after rugby and once again, his timing was perfect – leaving everyone who watched that team develop from 1966 to the day he left in 1970 with some special memories.

"He wasn't going to let a troublesome knee spoil that and I don't think there has been a player since who has played at full-back and left such a lasting impression in just four years.

"Later on, Bev was instrumental, along with Joe Warham and Ken Rollin in setting up the Leeds ex-Players Association which still keeps the friendships and memories alive of those special times."

I stayed at the club until the end of the season and delayed my knee operation until I had finished my studies at Leeds University.

I hobbled around watching all the matches with mixed emotions, trying to come to terms with the reality of retirement.

I knew I would miss the adrenalin rush of the matches and the competition and camaraderie with my team mates.

I believed I'd done everything possible as a player but I still had a driving intention to remain in the sport in some way and make a contribution to its development and evolution.

Little did I know how things would turn out but I could never have envisaged the path my life would follow and some of the extraordinary experiences I would be involved in including; organising a rugby league tour to exotic Morocco, being the technical director of a West End play about the game, transporting 120 students across to Australia for a World Cup, having a boss called Richard Branson in a role as director of development at London Broncos, and serving as president of the Rugby Football League for a year – all of which would culminate in going to Buckingham Palace to be awarded an honour for my work in rugby league.

None of that could have been foreseen as I faced a blank canvas in 1970, as a temporarily crippled ex-player and out of work teacher, I had to get my act together with a wife and three young sons to support.

First, I was determined to follow my original ambition to work in sport in a higher education environment.

Ann and I discussed the situation and we were quite flexible on where we might live but I had the feeling that having a complete break from rugby league might be a good idea and would enable us to have a more settled family life.

So I applied for a lecturing position in a number of colleges and universities, even considering moving to Australia or New Zealand.

Eventually I was offered a job at Berkshire College of Higher Education in Reading, I'm not sure we'd really thought about the implications of living in the south, not least how I would cope without my weekly dose of rugby league tonic.

I started in September so we had most of the summer to prepare for the move.

I took my masters exams and graduated successfully at Leeds University in June then had my first knee operation at Pinderfields Hospital Wakefield in July.

We sold our house on Baildon Moor and bought a property in Crowthorne, Berskshire at double the price.

We had to get used to the cost of living in the south, very quickly learning the meaning of the word 'gazumping'

The night before we moved, all the Leeds team and half the road came to our leaving do, staged around all our worldly possessions packed up in boxes.

We sang and danced and told stories of our exploits, it went on all night.

The highlight of the evening was when Alan Lockwood, our wily hooker, suddenly knocked loudly and appeared at the lounge door dressed as a hula-hula girl.

He had been rummaging through my memorabilia and wore the grass skirt, Maori headband and full Haka makeup that I'd been presented with on tour.

To complete the look, he'd been into the kitchen and snatched two full cream plastic trifle cases and stuck them over his nipples on his bare chest.

Whilst we howled at his appearance, he then announced: "I've just been sick down the toilet ... can you get my false teeth out for me."

We laughed even more wildly and I went for my rubber gloves.

The party went on until morning and we served toast and coffee to seemingly thousands on our little back lawn as the July sun came up over the Moor.

On the horizon we could see a shadowy figure wandering over towards us which quietened the guests somewhat, but it turned out to be the local shepherd who joined us with hilarious tales of his own.

It was a wonderful way to end our stay in Yorkshire.

The removal man packed our remaining boxes and furniture and we had a big wave off and cheer from the neighbours as we set off down the hill towards an uncertain future.

Ann drove our little Austin Minivan with the three boys bedded down in sleeping bags in the back while I went ahead leading the way in our Austin A40.

It's probably fair to say we departed our hilltop home in Yorkshire with an excited sense of adventure but a little trepidation.

We thought that we might spend two or three years away from the north at most but finished up staying for more than 30.

Our parents and family living in Cumbria believed we were going to the ends of the earth but the boys knew no other life and are still settled down there.

Ann and I never lost our northern roots and continued to plough up and down the motorways.

We maintained our friends and contacts and enjoyed holidays in the Lake District until we moved back up there again when Ann retired in 1999.

She had carved out a highly successful career in education and politics becoming the first female chair of Berkshire County Council.

At the same time, I developed new leisure interests and a number of outlets in my education work as I spread my wings into other fields.

But seeing my three sons grow up, watching them play in school and local teams, winning on sports days and at swimming galas, them making close friends and getting good school reports, was the bedrock of my own development and all that we both could have wished for.

At work in my new job, I found myself taking charge of the college rugby union team.

I was soon to discover, however, that there could be

problems with my league background in the 15-a-side hotbeds of London and the south.

I realised that I would have to tread warily even talking about my first love and that life would not be easy if I tried to develop rugby league and get involved with the emerging developments in the region.

I deliberately laid low for a while, settling in and soon found that, under the education umbrella, no-one seemed too concerned about my coaching students when, under strict rugby union regulations, I should have been banned.

Clearly, a blind eye was being turned and it was not long before I was asked to help with the British College representative team and finally England RU students, working with John Robbins.

It appeared that as long as I was only coaching student teams there was no problem, so I just carried on.

The English Students organisation was under the auspices of the RFU and it was only when I was nominated to represent them on the national committee that the line was drawn.

Robin Prescott, secretary of the RFU, and a good friend from my playing days wrote to me and suggested that it would be inappropriate for an ex-professional player to be appointed to the position.

Now, of course, in the fully professional era for both codes, union is full of former league people as players, administrators and coaches.

I eventually joined the British Rugby League Coaching Scheme led by Phil Larder and officially became the regional coach for the South.

An essential part of that role was working alongside the British Amateur Rugby League Association (BARLA) with stalwarts such as Cliff Buckton, secretary of London

ARL, Bob Evans and Tim Lamb. I was now working on both sides of the fence and really enjoying it.

The BRLCS at this time was the envy of sports coaching bodies throughout the country and Phil produced a coaching manual which became a bible in sport, way ahead of its time.

I had a major responsibility to spread the word and promote rugby league throughout the country, helping to staff all levels of courses both regionally and nationally.

We had an outstanding group of regional coaches including Clive Griffiths, Eric Fitzsimmons, Graeme Starkey, Dennis McHugh, John Kain and John Kear, who eventually took over from Phil as director of coaching, all of whom played and coached at professional level in the 1960s and 70s.

Through the scheme it was possible to work with dedicated people from grassroots level and players up to junior international standard.

One of my most memorable experiences was staffing a course at Lilleshall for our outstanding 16-year-olds which included future stars such as Phil Clarke and Denis Betts.

Phil Larder eventually became the Great Britain coach but he did not achieve the long term success and recognition in rugby league that he had hoped for and decided to move on to pastures new.

He crossed to union and was much more than just a defence coach, becoming an integral part of Sir Clive Woodward's coaching team that led England to their triumph in the 2003 RU World Cup in Australia.

In my opinion, he was a loss to league.

A New Life

13

I was only 33 when I retired at Leeds and I reckoned that, athletically at least, I still had many good years ahead of me in sport despite a couple of gammy knees.

I'd been happy to go out at the top professionally but now had to look for different, new challenges.

As a youngster, encouraged by Dad, I'd played almost everything and in some sports had reached a reasonably high level. Being a PE teacher then lecturer, I had to cover many of them which meant keeping my personal performance up to scratch and maintaining my fitness levels.

The first knee operation, cleaning out the joint and having the cartilage removed had been a complete success and I worked on my recovery without any problem.

I set myself personal targets and worked with the students on fitness projects, joining in as a subject in various experiments, participating in the athletics programme to build up my strength, speed and stamina.

Golf had always been a passion since Dad had given me a set of clubs when I was 11 years old and I soon reached a respectable handicap.

I joined the local club, which was only 100 yards from our house and was determined to get it down further.

I'd played tennis to county level and took part at junior Wimbledon so I had options there and I decided to take up squash, joining the team at nearby Wellington College.

All that was fine but I found that an essential ingredient was missing.

Although I was coaching rugby and soccer, I became very frustrated with not being involved with the unique camaraderie of a team sport.

I had always been, like so many others, a dreamer about playing for Manchester United, Bobby Charlton was my hero and being a left-footer myself, I rather fancied the idea of giving the round ball a go.

My sons were just starting to play and were looking good. I had to take an FA course to qualify to coach at the college and then started to help with the coaching and management at Finchampstead football club where all three boys eventually played.

I also joined a local club, Berkshire County Sports FC, who played in the Reading and District league Division 4 East and was determined to play regularly on a Saturday afternoon.

My only previous experience was when I was at university and occasionally turned out for Hulme Hall wearing a long sleeved shirt covering the plaster cast protecting my then broken wrist.

My last rugby match had been in front of 20,000 screaming fans at Warrington, the first soccer fixture six months later was on a local council park pitch in front of the bucket and sponge man and my wife, sitting on a travelling rug with our kids darting about trying to copy us.

I subsequently played for more than 11 years until I was 45, incidentally my dad's age when he finally retired from top class rugby league, and enjoyed every minute.

We won nothing but did get promotion to Division 2 and I only retired when the manager suggested that I might be better playing for the second team.

I started as a centre forward because I quickly found that most of my team mates had plenty of skill and talked a good game but little pace or strength at this level.

Relatively, I was quicker and stronger but as the seasons wore on I gradually retreated until I finished at left back where my main asset was to hoof the ball a long way thanks to my goal-kicking experience, and had to join the talkers rather than doers.

It was often muddy and the heavy leather ball was difficult to kick any distance so, quite often, I used to toe end it as was the rugby place-kicking technique in the 60s and 70s.

On one occasion, I collected the ball well in our own half and saw the opposing goalkeeper standing on the edge of the penalty area.

I took a good run up and, in my usual style, smashed the ball forward, it sailed over the goalie and into the net, I bent it almost like Beckham.

Over the next few years, I was able to improve my golf and squash with the help of some great friends.

When I met Bob Smitherman, a nine-stone marathon runner, fitness fiend, low handicap golfer and squash fanatic, I felt as if I was back in short trousers.

He was so ruthless, he wouldn't even concede a six-inch putt.

We became great pals and along with giant pilot Len

Amor, knocked lumps out of each other for many years, keeping our competitive edge and instinct razor sharp.

My sons were all starting their own sporting and academic lives and Ann and I spent much of our time driving them around, standing on touchlines and in athletics arenas, shouting ourselves hoarse in support.

The wheel had almost turned full circle for me.

Despite the threats of ex-communication, I secretly coached a couple of senior rugby union teams in the area to keep my hand in and received some generous travelling expenses for my efforts.

Like a homing pigeon, though, I eventually became part of the Student Rugby League committee under chairmanship of Martyn Sadler, as league rapidly became more popular in colleges and universities.

Having moved to West London Institute, day to day duties increasingly involved developing new degree courses in the field of teacher training.

On the academic and theoretical side, I wrote the CNAA Sports Studies syllabus and was responsible for practical elements, particularly in the sports of rugby, soccer, athletics, squash and tennis where students had the opportunity to improve both their performance and their teaching and coaching skills.

In my early days at Berkshire College of Higher Education, two unique opportunities arose.

Out of the blue, I was contacted by renowned film director Lindsay Anderson who was involved with author and playwright David Storey in a staging of his league-inspired play *The Changing Room* in the West End.

David and Lindsay had worked together some years before on the big hit film again based on league, *This Sporting Life* and Lindsay was doing similar with the stage.

He needed someone with rugby league experience to help with authenticity and as one of the few ex-pros living around London at the time, my name had been mentioned to them.

They wanted to see if I would be interested in the position of technical advisor and naturally I jumped at the chance even though, at the time, I didn't know what I was letting myself in for.

Wakefield-born miner's son David had shown promise as a player. He was signed by Leeds and played for the 'A' team for a couple of years but his passion for the arts meant that it was a means to end to get him through Slade Art College.

His play was a comedy drama about the goings on in a dressing room before during and after a match, and it was a critically acclaimed success.

After an abortive attempt to try to turn sportsman into actors, my task was to help turn actors into credible characters who looked and performed like rugby players.

A top quality cast was recruited including Warren Clarke, Mark McManus, Brian Glover, Edward Judd and Alun Armstrong.

To get them in character, Lindsay immediately insisted on placing the cast in the right environment.

He took everyone to a rugby club in West London and asked me to organise a seven-a-side match between the players and actors, to simulate the feel and atmosphere.

It was supposed to be touch-and-pass but very quickly turned into a free for all, full-on contact confrontation with no holds barred.

I was terrified that someone was going to get seriously injured because most of the actors had little skills but no fear.

It had the desired effect as the typical feelings of effort, physicality and after-match exhaustion they were trying to convey now had some meaning.

In reality, most players quickly got changed and into the action but the first act was around 45 minutes and I had to teach them all the intricacies; undressing, fiddling with their kit, boots, shorts, laces, jock straps, shirts, shoulder pads, strapping, massage, warm ups and stretching plus make it seem as though it was in real time.

At the same time all the conversation, banter and eccentricities of individual players – the quick smoke in the corner or a swig of sherry – had to be incorporated and believable.

We had an intense three weeks trying to perfect the individual antics of each actor prior to the first performance in the famous Royal Court Theatre.

The play was an amazing success with great reviews and afterwards moved on to the Globe and eventually, with an American production, to Newhaven and Broadway itself.

It was hailed as a landmark not only for rugby with all its inherent drama but also for the display of full frontal nudity which came as something of a surprise to the audience, not least Ann who had thoughtfully been given a front row seat for the first night.

Twenty-five years later, the play was chosen by theatre critics as one of the most outstanding and original performed in the West End.

I had the great good fortune to be asked back joining David Storey, Lindsay Anderson and an entirely new cast to recreate it.

Around the same time as the play first ran, I also became heavily involved in tennis.

The Lawn Tennis Association was awash with money

mainly as a result of the vast profits made from the Wimbledon Championships and looked to broaden its upper and middle-class base whilst also attempting to incorporate the latest training methods.

My work was with the best British players, from eight-year-old juniors to the top adult players in the country, and particularly in their preparation for tournaments and the prestigious Davis Cup.

I was able to fit it in as a second job with my lecturing commitments and my appointment was a new role working with the director of coaching and Davis Cup captain, Paul Hutchins.

The new national training centre was based at Bisham Abbey, no more than fifteen minutes from home and my experience in cutting-edge fitness training and coaching combined with playing tennis to a reasonably high standard, and rugby internationally, persuaded Paul to offer me the post.

In the 1970s, the importance of fitness training was just starting to be recognised and part of my job was to convince reluctant but quality players of all ages that the sport was no longer just about chasing a ball around a court.

I had to plan a programme designed to improve their fitness levels specific to tennis and also supervise, when possible given their commitments, individual and group training sessions.

Tennis is an extremely technical, skilled sport but there was now an added need for strength, speed, agility and stamina to compete with the world's best emerging at the time.

Certain players took some convincing.

The Davis Cup squad at the time was John and David Lloyd, Buster Mottram and Mark Cox, later joined by Richard

Lewis and Jeremy Bates. David was initially quite reluctant to include specific fitness work in his regime.

Under my supervision in the build-ups to Davis Cup matches and weekly camps for juniors, they all worked enthusiastically but left to their own devices, fitness training was still last on their list of priorities away from my eagle-eye.

I had the good fortune during ten years or more with the LTA to mix with all the greatest players at national and international tournaments.

It also began a great friendship with Richard Lewis that carried on when he became chief executive at the Rugby Football League, a post I recommended to him.

"As a junior tennis player I watched a match at the Albert Hall where top American player Clark Graebner suffered cramp and was in agony out on court," Richard remembers.

"He battled for over an hour before finally losing and in that moment I vowed to be so fit that I never cramped up during a game.

"Wanting to be fit was one thing, knowing how to do it was another. My experience of training up until that point was a couple of intensive weeks at the Lilleshall National Sports Centre where the expertise available left the players in such a state that the only way to get downstairs was backwards, so stiff were we from the previous days training.

"Nobody had heard of lactic acid in those days so when Bev was to be the Davis Cup team trainer I, for one, was delighted.

Richard adds: "His knowledge, experience and people skills made sure peak fitness was achieved through applying sound sports science without going through unnecessary pain.

"From my first encounters with him, it was obvious there was something about Bev, he instilled confidence through his quiet, unassuming but direct and knowledgeable manner.

"Here is a man that you did not argue with, he just exuded sincerity and calmness that made you believe in him and made you want to go to your limits for him.

"You felt that you were in the presence of greatness and, of course, you were.

"It was a thrill when I joined the RFL in 2002 to be reunited with him.

"He was one of the first people I met following my appointment and it was apparent that even in the sport where he excelled, modesty was to the fore, he is so understated in what he loves but extremely impressive when you get to know him."

The gospel that I was spreading is now commonplace in the sport as exemplified by the likes of Djokovic, Murray, Nadal and Federer and I'd like to believe that I played a part in the change of attitudes to fitness here.

I became heavily involved in improvements in coaching and had some responsibility, with Charles Applewhaite who took over from Paul, in producing the new coaching manual of the time.

I also initiated and edited a new magazine called Coaches and Coaching, and even thought for a while of taking a full-time position at the LTA and leaving lecturing.

Sport-related fitness became an area of expertise and, in the 1980s, when I was at West London, I became involved in a new programme aimed at extending the idea to the general public.

Debate centred upon what type of exercise was necessary in order to bring about an improvement in health.

The *Sunday Times* took up the clarion call for more research to be carried out in the field and sponsored a major study on the subject.

They asked for volunteers to be subjects of a year-long exercise programme during which they would be regularly examined in a whole range of anatomical, physiological and medical tests to calculate the effects.

It was called 'Getting in Shape' and was also endorsed by the Sports Council and the Health Education Council. Nearly 200 subjects between the ages of 35 and 55, who had done little or no exercise for a number of years, were chosen.

Their medical condition was assessed regularly by Professor David Dennison, a famous clinical physiologist and his staff at the renowned Brompton Hospital.

My colleague Malcolm Emery and his student assistants at the West London Institute monitored the anatomical and exercise elements. My responsibility was to design and coordinate an exercise programme to be carried out throughout the year, which was equivalent to two, two-hour sessions per week.

Almost unbelievably, over 90 per cent of the subjects completed the course and there were regular updates in the newspaper by journalist Geoffrey Canon who kept the readers informed throughout about the project and its participants.

It was a highly rewarding experience to be involved in as part of a team conducting extremely important research.

Back to my Roots

14

I didn't suffer any sort of mid-life crisis but in my mid-40s, I started thinking about what I was going to do for the rest of my life.

Ann was working full-time and also becoming heavily involved in local politics, she had also studied for a masters in philosophy at Nottingham University and gained an advanced diploma in adult education at London University.

Our sons initially gained scholarships to Wellington College and were doing well in their studies and sport.

All three progressed to University and got their degrees; Martin went to Loughborough, loved his rugby and played for Surrey, Camberley, Guildford and Chobham in a 15-year career, and as an ace goal-kicker, scored over 3000 points, more than I ever did.

John studied at Oxford and won Blues at rugby – the first to get them at both union and league – and athletics.

He played for England students at union and would undoubtedly have gone on to higher things had he not irretrievably damaged his knee ligaments playing for Richmond.

Both he and Martin are now single figure golfers and John is a fitness fanatic constantly cycling and doing triathlons.

Michael played for England Colts RU and got Blues in both rugby and athletics at Cambridge.

Although he played union for a while for Rosslyn Park, his ambitions took him to America and Harvard for his MBA.

When he returned, the 15-a-side game was embracing professionalism and his career path took him to the City.

I felt I had gone as far as I could in higher education and it was being suggested that I was ready for a desk job, couched in terms of a promotion, it didn't really appeal so I started to re-examine my options.

I'd also become slightly disillusioned having proposed a restructuring of the academic programme at West London Institute to establish the college as one of the major schools of sport in the country.

Others decided differently, so I reckoned it was time to move on and took up the opportunity of voluntary redundancy.

Nagging away at me all the time was the thought of unfinished business and a return to rugby league which seemed, inevitably, to mean a move back north.

In the mid-70s, when I'd only been in the real world for a couple of years, the then secretary of the RFL, Bill Fallowfield, retired.

The sport was in the doldrums as regards crowds and commercial appeal and it was a rare opportunity to take it in a new direction after Bill's rod of iron approach, which had had its successes.

Change was in the air and, on paper, I had all the qualifications needed and decided to apply for his job.

I really thought that I had at least some of the answers and could make a difference and leave my mark on the game.

I was installed as a hot favourite and, amidst much subterfuge, was more or less assured by Brian Snape who was on the interview panel that the job was mine.

However, along came an unknown, Hull-born, public school deputy headmaster, David Oxley, whose silver tongue convinced the directors that he was the ideal for the role.

David takes up the story. "I first met Bev one blustery April Day just before Easter 1974. The venue was what passed as a waiting room at the RFL's then headquarters at 180 Chapeltown Road in Leeds.

"I, along with Bev and Ron Bailey, a highly regarded part-time secretary at Featherstone Rovers and a senior officer of the National Coal Board, were the final shortlisted candidates being interviewed to succeed Bill.

"The formidable decision makers comprised the current chairman of the RFL, Ronnie Simpson assisted by chairman-elect Brian Snape, the immediate past chairman, Hubert Lockwood of Huddersfield and other former chairs including Tom Mitchell (Workington), Arthur Walker (Oldham), Jim Davies (Widnes), John Jepson (Featherstone), Wilf Sparks (Hull KR), Jack Harding (Leigh) and John Smallwood (Keighley).

"There is absolutely no doubt that given Bev's immaculate pedigree and Ron's experience I was the rank outsider.

"As a consequence, I felt no nerves during the interview and with nothing to lose expressed in very strong terms exactly what I thought about the current state of the game and what needed to be done to put it right.

"In the event, the panel came down for reasons only known to themselves on my side."

David confirms: "It is true that at that time the great game was not in good shape. The standard of play was ordinary, the crowds were shrinking alarmingly, BARLA – formed in 1973 – had effectively broken away from the RFL and morale was at a low ebb.

"Indeed the loyal and very efficient assistant secretary, Eddie Bottomley in welcoming me to HQ said that he could not understand why I had accepted the job since, 'none of us will have one in a year's time.'"

Losing out was a real sickener, I was left to stew for several days and it was only when I contacted the RFL to find out what was happening that I was told that David had got the job.

It took me a long time to get over the way I had been treated, but I never lost my enthusiasm for league and, much later than I anticipated, found my way back into the game.

In the meantime, David did a magnificent job of putting the sport back on its feet, skilfully overcoming a number of crises on the way.

He appointed able lieutenants, David Howes as front man and Geoff Keith administratively behind the scenes, with considerable help and support from powerful chairmen Sir Rodney Walker, Bob Ashby and later the charismatic Maurice Lindsay.

I'd kept my contacts and fate again intervened just as I was pursuing possible further involvement with tennis.

Much as I enjoyed the work, there was a lingering thought it might steer me into a limiting corner, which I was somewhat reluctant about.

Also, my friend and colleague at West London Institute, Malcolm Emery was setting up a fitness and health clinic in Harley Street and dangled the carrot of a six-week visit to Abu Dhabi to be personal trainer to a well-known Sheikh for a fee of £50,000 with the potential of more to come.

In the end, I decided that the most exciting venture would be to keep all the balls in the air by setting up my own business as a coaching and fitness consultant and try to enjoy the best of several worlds.

I was able to do more coaching and development work for rugby league in the south, much of it as a labour of love but very rewarding for me personally.

Then, in 1987, came the offer of managing Fulham RLFC and my involvement in the sport was back on track.

In 1980, a rugby league bombshell hit the capital with the creation of a professional club playing at Craven Cottage and named Fulham RLFC like their soccer landlords

It was the brainchild of Australian Harold Genders and fully supported by Ernie Clay, the chairman of the soccer club, and championed by Colin *'Chariots of Fire'* Welland.

Harold got the okay from the Rugby League Council and put a team together in a matter of weeks, recruiting a squad of 'mercenaries' mainly from the North West to join the Second Division newcomers.

The first match was against the mighty but then sleeping giants Wigan and history was created when Fulham amazingly won the game and attracted a 10,000 plus crowd, many of whom knew little about league, some spectators even clapping knock-ons!

Well-known names such as Roy Lester and giant forwards Harry Beverley, Ian van Bellen and John Wood, high class backs David Eckersley, Mal Aspey, my brother John and ace goal-kicker Ian McCorquodale were all signed.

Tony Karalius and player/coach Reg Bowden ruled the midfield and raw recruits Welsh winger Adrian Cambriani and back rower Martin Herdman, the first player to come from the capital to don the shirt and now an actor, soon made their mark.

A quick death was forecast for the initiative but the critics were confounded when Fulham won promotion in their first season in front of healthy attendances, beating Leeds in the John Player Cup along the way and drawing over 15,000 fans when they played Wakefield in the Challenge Cup.

I wondered whether I should offer my services in some capacity but was heavily engrossed in my work at the time and was never asked to join even though I was involved with the coaching scheme and amateur game in London.

It was the start of what could have been a monumental success story for the sport in the capital and I watched the developments with great anticipation fervently hoping it would be much more than a one season wonder.

Success on the field was everything in order to maintain spectator interest and establish a sound support base, but after instant promotion and despite valiant efforts in the First Division, Fulham were relegated and the momentum was lost.

The finance dried up, the soccer club lost its enthusiasm, there was no local player development pathway and the Northerners began to tire of the monotonous trips up and down the motorway.

The club took on a nomadic existence and although the name stayed the same, changes of venue did nothing to maintain support and interest. It had been a great adventure but was doomed to ultimate failure, Fulham eventually finding their way to the Chiswick Polytechnic Ground.

Barbara and Roy Close had taken over the ailing club with some token help from the RFL but by this time they were doing little more than surviving.

To their credit they managed to keep it going despite little on field success.

I had always held strong views about what was required to create long term stability for the sport in London after repeated failures and the opportunity arose for me to test the water when I was eventually given the position of team manager, after previously working as an advisor.

I was to have an unofficial three year, part-time contract and the plan was to promote a long-term development strategy at all age levels so that, over time, the bulk of the side would be made up of locals with only a smattering of incomers to provide the necessary experience.

There was nothing too revolutionary about this but in the absence of a 'sugar daddy,' it was the only sensible way forward.

We gathered together a group of rugby league stalwarts, some of whom had been at the club through thick and thin such as Tim Lamb and Bob Evans, Barbara Close as chair and Roy leading the way off the field.

Bill Goodwin and the ever-faithful Paul Johnstone worked with me on the coaching side, it was great to be part of a group of people who were passionate about the game in London and prepared to work tirelessly to achieve success.

We had facilities as good as most second division clubs at Chiswick with ample changing rooms, an excellent pitch and a floodlit training ground.

We started to recruit local players from the amateur London League ranks, until then, amazingly, Frank Feighan apart, none had been deemed good enough during the Harold Genders era.

Bill and Paul had all the necessary knowledge working with teams in the area and we started our plan by inviting anyone with ambitions to play for Fulham to turn up in the pre-season before the 1987-88 campaign.

Eventually, we had over fifty players regularly attending and there was even talk of running an 'A' team and it seemed everyone bought into our new endeavour, players, coaches, directors and supporters were all prepared to give it a go – at least on the surface.

There were problems with some London League clubs who wanted to preserve status in their competition, but the opportunity for these lads to play professionally and compete at a higher level fuelled their desire to see how far they could progress in the sport.

Some very promising youngsters were quick to join, quality rugby union players such as Huw Rees and Keiron Murphy committed themselves and top amateurs including Dave Gillan, Mick Hutchinson, Nick Grimoldby, Colin Fenn and Steve Guyett relished the opportunity along with some quality students including Russ Bridge and Dave Rotheram.

Australians Glen Haggarth, a top class professional and Pat O'Docherty a young dynamic prop, were recruited and others appeared out of the woodwork to help bring on the amateurs.

We built a reasonable side that grew in confidence but unfortunately the improvement did not materialise quickly enough at the start of the next season and certain factions on the committee lost patience and confidence.

My three year development plan was shelved and very brief sojourn into professional team coaching came to an abrupt end as I was shown the door in favour of a more pragmatic approach, which they hoped would bring better results.

But the club continued to struggle along, Bill Goodwin took over the coaching reins and I watched the events unfold from the outside.

I am still convinced that my philosophy was the correct way forward but other influential figures thought they knew better.

At the time I was shocked and disappointed but left for pastures new to pursue a totally different direction in the game.

I had time to spare because my sons were now starting on their careers in business, Ann had been their anchor while I was travelling about constantly and was now developing her own career path in Adult Education.

A new development programme for rugby league in the south was starting to emerge under the auspices of Tom O'Donovan at the RFL and the post of London development officer was advertised and I decided to apply.

I wasn't sure if my views coincided with those of the governing body but an interview would at least give me the chance to express my opinions.

To my surprise, when I turned up for it, RFL chairman Bob Ashby had other ideas and decided that, as I was still on the SRL committee, I would be perfect to organise the 1989 Student World Cup.

In an international board meeting, he had volunteered to host it and now needed someone to organise the event.

He enquired if I would take it on a nine month appointment and I immediately got very excited at the thought of such a major challenge but I needed a regular full-time job.

I asked Bob if he would consider appointing me as director of the SRL on a three year contract with my first duty to organise the tournament.

He agreed, with the proviso that the event was successful, I accepted and embarked on one of the most exciting experiences of my life in league.

Having been a member of the SRL committee for several years, I knew most of the ins and outs and how ambitious members of it were to see the student sector in the forefront of the sport's development.

The organisation had become an integral part of the RFL after its initial connection with BARLA and limited funding was provided by the Rugby League Foundation.

The SRL organised competitions and fixtures among twenty-four or so institutions and also planned a representative programme of international matches and student inter-sector competitions.

Everyone recognised the value of a potentially thriving student game for spreading the sport and opening it up to future leaders in the commercial world, but we were hamstrung by a shortage of funding and one of my main duties was to try to rectify that.

I was determined to make a success of my new appointment looking to promote and develop the student game using the World Cup as a stepping stone to greater things for the game.

As it turned out, I remained in post until retiring in 1995 and was fortunate to oversee a massive expansion in the student sector with over seventy universities, colleges and polytechnics competing in a comprehensive structure, with an ever expanding representative and international programme and another World Cup in Australia in 1992.

Initially, I travelled far and wide throughout Britain to promote the game, from Exeter to Aberdeen, all over London, Oxford and Cambridge, Newcastle, Bangor and over to Ireland.

More teams sprang up in the heartland areas of Lancashire, Yorkshire and Cumbria and in the Midlands too. New countries were brought in to the fold for the 1989 World Cup which involved eight nations; England, Wales, Scotland, Ireland, Australia, New Zealand, France and, amazingly, a team from Holland.

David Oxley, in charge at the RFL was tremendously supportive. "Australia just pipped England 10-4 in an epic final played at Central Park Wigan, and the culminating gala dinner, attended by over 400 people, included a series of acts of a typically national nature by each competing team," he says.

"The whole joyous evening was brought to a remarkable conclusion when the exuberant Lady Mayor of Wigan performed an energetic clog dance on the top table.

"After this triumph it was almost inevitable that Bev would be invited to become the SRL's first full-time director and the succeeding seven years were a golden age for our game at University level

"Between 1989 and 1996 the number of universities playing rugby league more than doubled, Bev recruiting on average five new sides every year from his office at Oxford's famous Iffley Road arena, the setting for Roger Bannister's historic first sub four minute mile run in 1954.

"In a characteristic and innovative flurry of activity, he established the SRL as a limited company and set up the structures on which the student game is now so firmly established.

"In national leagues, Super 8s, regional competitions, merit tables, representative festivals, the annual Four Nations championships, regular international matches and frequent incoming and outgoing tours – especially visiting Australia – the standard of play has improved beyond measure."

I was the only paid officer but had an impressive band of dedicated volunteers and particularly Martyn Sadler and David Oxley who served as chairmen, together with unstinting workers Tim Butcher, Simon Adamson, Mark Brierley, Niel Tunnicliffe and Malcolm Reid who led the Scottish initiative.

Phil Melling and Dannie and Keri Sheehy did likewise in Wales and Brian Corrigan and Niel Wood in Ireland.

We were fortunate to have skilled help from high level coaches including ex-referee Fred Lindop at Sheffield, Mike Penistone and John Kain with the international squad and numerous others at club level who were interested to work with eager raw material.

Most important, too, was the band of around 50 referees who loved the student game and travelled nationwide to ensure that all fixtures were fulfilled.

Part of my role was to organise the appointments schedule for Wednesday and Sunday matches and every midweek morning I waited anxiously to see if anyone cried off so that I could combine my weekly visit to a game with refereeing duties which I loved.

I couldn't be happier with the way SRL has developed since then, Niel Wood subsequently taking over.

He remembers the handover.

"The 1989 World Cup was great fun, inspirational and truly significant in the history of the sport – the first event to have true multi-national involvement," he recalls.

"In 1992 Bev again lead us into again and once more his calm and unflustered appraoch got a hundred students across the globe and back again largely in one piece, which in itself is no mean feat.

"I remember him making his way to Canberra to sort

out a missing passport, done with fantastic grace when I would have been thinking 'bloody students.'"

"The opportunity to take over from him, with everything that he'd established and all the relationships he had built up was too good to be true.

"The transition was simple and typical, he advised 'get a decent car because you will spend hours in it.'"

He adds: "Following Bev was the easiest job in the world, he had set everything up and walked away leaving his blessing, no interference yet a telephone number to ring at any time for help and advice.

"If Student rugby league stands for anything, it's dealing in a calm, intelligent and sympathetic manner without getting carried away with a sense of its own self-importance.

"As a student you learn that some things are really important and others are meant to be fun, which makes the fun more important. Bev captured that and passed it on to me and thousands of others."

The Best of Both Worlds

15

Suddenly, in 1995, rugby league was blown wide open with the creation of Super League.

The decision to have full-time players was revolutionary and I decided to take a leap into the unknown.

I'd thought my time had come to take a back seat at the age of 59 and had a readymade successor to me at the SRL.

Out of the blue, the latest incarnation of what had been Fulham, the new London Broncos club appeared on the scene and Australian entrepreneur Barry Maranta, assisted by his son Michael, took over the running of it and they were given a place in Super League.

Barry was the chairman and owner of the Brisbane Broncos, the drivers of the new competition in Australia who had been looking for an opportunity to play a part in the adventure here.

The professional club in London, then known before

the upgrade as the Crusaders, was struggling along in Division 2 and had no permanent home.

They'd made a fleeting appearance in the divisional final, losing against Workington Town at Old Trafford, their best performance since the Craven Cottage days at Fulham.

There was little cash available to keep the Crusaders going and it was a great credit to all concerned over the years that they had survived for so long.

Now the cash-rich Brisbane Broncos had come along.

The decision to have a London presence in Super League, sidestepping traditional promotion, was not unanimously accepted by the other clubs and Barry asked me if I would join the Broncos as their director of development with a seat on the board.

I'd been on the road for seven years and decided that the post would be perfect and allow me to spend more time at home.

It also felt as if the sport was finally making a sustainable breakthrough in London with a well-financed top flight club tapping into some serious expertise and providing a high level focal point for all the enthusiasts in the area.

Work in the schools was expanding rapidly under the RFL junior development programme and providing the chance for enthusiastic children to take part in the sport.

The efforts of development officers was working as more amateur teams were being formed, and there was a new air of excitement in the region.

I decided that my best contribution would be to concentrate on the elite area of the game at junior level.

The objective would be to recruit youngsters with potential and produce Broncos squads at different age levels to compete against similar teams from the professional clubs and other newer areas.

My aim was to generate a conveyor belt of local and regional talent starting at U16s, through an U18 Academy, into U21s and hopefully, eventually to Super League standard, that was the magnet.

We entered the National Academy League and competed alongside such as Leeds and Wigan, it was a high risk strategy because the target had to be young rugby union players already performing at a high level which was bound to make waves.

But it was instantly encouraging to see how many were prepared to try their hand at league particularly as the sport had moved to summer and that lessened potential conflict between the codes.

Despite some union resistance we got together a squad of over 40 players, my recruitment team searched far and wide and also explored players of union representative standard from Wales, Ireland and Scotland.

We even sneaked in to watch the emerging Johnny Wilkinson but decided that his game did not suit league!

Our first recruits included Matt Salter, Giles Thomas, Simon Amor and Kieron Campbell.

Matt and Giles made a success of the game, appearing in Super League and Kieron and Simon returned to union at representative level.

For the start of the 1996 Super League season, our squad was bolstered by seven academy-age players from Australia to give them a life experience and ensure that we could compete at the necessary level.

In our first season we finished a highly creditable sixth and our Australians Mickey Brown, Leroy Leapai, Mickey Janus and especially Tony Martin made an invaluable contribution, and helped our raw recruits to adjust to their new rugby league life.

Over the next two years matches were played as curtain raisers before Super League fixtures in the main stadium, a terrific experience for the youngsters to play at Charlton and Harlequins.

Tony Martin stayed on and signed a full-time contract, playing 34 matches for the Broncos before returning to Australia and New Zealand where he had a long and glittering career.

We had established ourselves and then worked to develop our younger age groups.

Alongside, an U21 Alliance team emerged for Super League players on the margins and aspiring ex-Academy performers.

Finally, an U16 squad was formed to compete in the national league.

Over 70 players turned up for our next pre-season trials at Crystal Palace Sports Centre which was the training base for all the squads.

The players seemed to be from every possible background and education and, notably, 60 per cent were black.

Typical was Ezekial May, a Rastafarian who was incredibly quick and elusive.

He approached me at the first trial to proudly announce that he had an attitude problem, couldn't stand being tackled nor resist getting into fights both at school and on the rugby field.

I told him that the first time he started fighting he would be cut from the squad and that I was offering him the chance of a lifetime.

He had a few near misses but eventually came through and played for the U16, Academy and Alliance teams very successfully.

He qualified in our apprenticeship scheme – students studying full-time for a NVQ in Sport and Leisure at Ann's Adult and Community college in Richmond, while training and playing at the Broncos – and stayed with the club for four years, only just missing out on a full-time contract.

The U16 squad was very talented and conquered all before them in the first season, finishing top of their regional group and winning immediate promotion.

The greatest triumph was at Bradford where we thrashed a team including a future star, Leon Pryce.

Our most successful students were Peter Lupton and Darrell Griffin who both went on to have very successful careers in Super League and all our first 23 students qualified for their NVQ Level 3, despite a number having no GCSE's.

Some went on to do degree courses and others continued to represent the Broncos or semi-professional side London Skolars and other newly established summer Rugby League Conference clubs.

The talent conveyor belt was quickly established and I put together an enthusiastic staff and volunteers who revelled in the new opportunities created by our work.

Dave Evans was development manager particularly of the apprentices, Dave Rotheram and Darryl Pitt ran the academy and Phil Jones coached the younger players and dealt with recruitment.

Our volunteers were physio Connor Gisagne, Mike Fox on the management side and Lee Toulson and the guru Steve McGee, maintenance manager supreme for all teams.

Later, my friend Graeme Thompson, came on board to strengthen the development team.

"I first came across Bev in 1994 at the Home Nations Student Championships in Aberavon although I didn't realise it was our first meeting initially!" Graeme recalls.

"Although very new to rugby league at the time, I was aware of the Risman dynasty as his brother John, was our Scotland Students head coach.

"Coming from union, I was particularly fascinated hearing about Bev, a captain of Britain at both sports and I looked forward to meeting the man of such remarkable achievements.

"I was sent down by the team management to collect some training kit from the tournament organisers.

"I duly did so and a man gave me the necessary apparel and at the same time we got talking about both codes.

"I returned to deliver the kit and someone enquired if I had met Bev. 'No,' I replied but I did meet this smallish bloke who seemed very well informed. Who knew?

Graeme continues: "And that's the thing about Bev for me, you would never necessarily know about his past achievements because, whenever I had the fortune to work for and with him, he never sought to use his playing credentials as his rationale for the natural status that accompanies his well-informed thoughts.

"He gave me a job at London Broncos in the late 1990s. There he had built up a significant youth programme and when I moved to the RFL performance department, he was there doing some consultancy work and was able to give me continued career guidance.

"Even in his 'retirement' I continue to benefit from his advice and experience.

"One aspect that always stands out about Bev is his belief in education and his skill of trying to directly or indirectly help people to improve themselves."

The Broncos was now a great success story and a golden era lay ahead at Super League and junior level.

The recruitment of quality players mainly from

abroad, such as Terry Matterson, Peter Gill, Steele Retchless, Great Britain tourist Tulsen Tollett, Tony Mestrov, Robbie Beasley, Rusty Bowden, Matt Toshack, John Timu and Kevin Langer, provided the base for senior team success.

Stalwarts from the pre-summer days like Steve Rossolen and Scott Roskell were still around and Rob Smyth, Karle Hammond, Jon Clarke came down from the north.

The first southerners came through in Matt Salter and then Ady Spencer, who took on the might of the RFU by playing for Cambridge in their Varsity match before being banned for appearing in a league shirt.

Scotland international Nick Mardon, Iain Higgins and Dom Peters, all locals, had success with the resurgent Broncos.

Robbie Moore came over from Brisbane Broncos to manage the club and former Leeds and Kangaroo centre Tony Currie was recruited as first team coach.

Tony Rea started as a player, became an administrator, was appointed CEO and subsequently coach over several seasons.

I continued in my role as director of development and enjoyed seeing our home products coming through to challenge for places in the senior squads.

Everything was running smoothly for our junior sections and the schools programme was rapidly expanding.

We had top-line sponsors with oil magnate David Hughes and Fosters via Keith Hogg and then, ultimately, the three-year reign of Richard Branson's Virgin company guided by Ian Burroughs and Brad Rosser.

The first team was making waves, major successes at that time was second place in Super League, beating Canberra Raiders in the World Challenge and appearing in the 1999 Challenge Cup final against Leeds.

The team were lead out for the last match at the old Wembley by an open-necked, shirt-sleeved, jeans-wearing Richard Branson, it was an iconic moment for the sport in the south.

Leeds took the honours that day but it was a magnificent achievement for the Broncos to reach those heights in such a short time, the team including two modern day legends of the game, Shaun Edwards and Martin Offiah.

There was now a wonderful chance for the Broncos to move on to bigger and better things and I felt that my time there was coming to an end.

The junior programme was well established with a number of local academy players challenging for places in the senior team. My aim had been to leave the legacy of a largely British academy team had been achieved, I had a natural successor in Dave Evans to take over my role and anyway, my long-suffering knees were starting to collapse.

Richard Branson's sponsorship was drawing to a close and I wrote him a letter and along with others, tried to persuade him to continue his sponsorship.

Without him the financial position was looking much less promising with cutbacks being proposed.

I argued that if he extended his deal now that the club was enjoying some success, it could become one of the forces in the game.

I had a meeting with Ian Burrows, one of his senior managers, but it was obvious that Richard had committed himself for three years and would now be moving on.

The young players on the cusp needed the encouragement of a full-time contract and I felt at this time that not enough of them were being given the financial encouragement they deserved to continue their rugby league careers.

There needed to be more integration and quality coaching alongside the senior players and some greater exposure to the first team squad.

Around 200 players by this time had come through the system with varying success, the twenty-three 16 and 17-year-old trainees were well looked after but those next up from the academy needed more encouragement and opportunities in my opinion.

The option was either to sign a full-time, established professional at £70,000 or to continue to fund seven promising apprentices at £10,000 each.

Although a greater risk, I obviously preferred to back giving the young ex-academy players some expert coaching to bring them through, but I lost the argument.

Nevertheless, I enjoyed my four years at the Broncos immensely and started something which is still going today.

Players are continually emerging from their junior ranks but as the Broncos are not now the force they were, the better players have moved to other clubs in Super League.

It is great to see Louie McCarthy-Scarsbrook, Dan Sarginson, Tony Clubb, Mike McMeeken *et al* carving out successful careers in the game.

The Broncos have struggled on field since, despite the sterling efforts and finances of David Hughes.

They failed to attract the necessary additional sponsorship when financial support from the funding bodies was very much reduced, meaning a loss of development officers in the region – although the setting up of a London Rugby League Foundation is aimed at addressing that.

The basic infrastructure remains in the region and large numbers of potential players are still participating in the area.

However, I felt that a once in a lifetime opportunity

was missed in the late 1990s and can only hope that further initiatives can be created to resurrect the club in the future.

Before I left the Broncos there was a major initiative in the amateur game in areas outside the sport's geographical strongholds.

A group of enthusiasts, including me, under the auspices of Tom O'Donovan the RFL's national development officer, decided to explore the possibilities of introducing summer rugby and looking at sharing facilities with community union clubs.

It was regarded with some scepticism within the amateur body BARLA but, nonetheless, an action group including Lionel Hurst, Hector McNeil, Julian Harrison and myself was formed which was later to include Trevor Moss, Neil Tunnicliffe, Graeme Thompson and Phil Caplan.

There were several official and unofficial meetings which included the RFL and BARLA and, after considerable discussion and prevarication, agreement was finally reached and an administrative structure set up with the indefatigable Harry Jepson elected as president and, ultimately, a trophy in his name.

In 1997, a pilot season involving 10 clubs from non-traditional areas; Leicester Phoenix, Birmingham Bulldogs, Worcester Royals, Oxford Cavaliers, Bedford Swifts, North London Skolars, Ipswich Rhinos, Cambridge Eagles and Kingston was organised, and from there the RLC set up eventually had over 150 clubs spread nationwide and covering Wales and Scotland.

It was an amazing achievement, matching the similar emergence of the Student Rugby League years before and was noted by MP David Hinchliffe.

"Bev's contribution to sport, and especially to rugby league, has been only partly about his undoubted abilities on the field," he says. "I think it can be seriously argued that his off-field advocacy of the game – and of the wider importance of sport in society – has, at the very least, equalled his brilliant on-field achievements.

"As someone who has always believed in the importance of expanding the sport beyond its northern heartlands, I can honestly say that there are few – if any – who deserve more credit for the progress made, in the south of England in particular, than Bev.

"In underlining his contribution, it must, of course, be remembered that his involvement in the development of the game in the south and in the organisation of student rugby league, took place for much of the time against a background of rugby union's discrimination against even amateur league players.

"It is often forgotten that union bans on league players only ended as recently as 1995."

David continues: "I first got to know Bev personally when the Parliamentary Rugby League Group began a political battle for the free movement of players between both codes.

"With his background in both and great respect throughout British sport, he was a wonderful ally in this ultimately successful campaign.

"He articulated a passionate personal belief in sport as a force for good in society in which outdated class divisions and attitudes of the past should have no place.

"When I wrote a book in 2000 which recorded the struggle for free movement, Bev did me the honour of speaking at its London launch.

"Present that night in Westminster were others who had similarly fought the rugby league cause in the south over many years."

Both Sides of the Fence

I took a back seat once the Rugby League Conference had been established but kept my involvement as chairman, coach and bucket carrier for the newly formed West London Sharks and later, after retiring back to Cumbria, served as chairman of Carlisle Centurions.

Back in the Lakes, I had one other last throw of the dice in league when I helped out with the Cumbria development programme for a short while.

What I thought might occupy six months turned into three years and during that time I tried to knock heads together at Workington and Whitehaven to explore the potential of a Cumbrian Super League club.

Despite valiant efforts and much good will and help from the RFL, I came up against the brick wall of local parochial interests.

I have every respect for individual opinion but no one was prepared to take the bull by the horns despite the potential support from the Allerdale and Copeland councils for a new community stadium, so that was that.

After a great 62 year innings in rugby, I was honoured in 2010 to be elected president of the RFL, especially having no specific club affiliation which had been the previous rule.

During my year of office, I visited Australia and New Zealand for the Four Nations championship, became a trustee of the Rugby League Cares charity and in the New Year's Honours list was awarded the OBE for my services to the sport, one of my proudest moments and not without some humour.

Our sons and I had been to Buckingham Palace when Ann received her OBE from HM the Queen for services to Further Education in 1999. Mine was presented by HRH Prince Charles who is much respected and admired in Cumbria for his staunch support of the rural community.

Knowing how well prepared he always is, I half expected that he might refer to the Cumbrian connection in the few words allowed as the award is given but not a bit of it.

"That's a very rough game you've been playing, I see," said the Prince, with a twinkle in his eye. "Did you ever get injured?"

"I am afraid so Sir," I replied with a broad grin and began my list. "Two new knees, broken wrist, broken leg, broken jaw, broken nose, stitched up forehead, throttled throat, several bouts of concussion..."

"Stop," laughed the Prince. "That's enough."

And he was right.

The New Rugby

16

I've spent my lifetime in rugby, on both sides of the fence that still exists between league – my first love – and union.

Whether paid or not, the complexities, tensions and pitfalls of being deeply involved at a high level in either of the two codes are worth recounting.

They are common to all of us who have gone down this path; injuries, media pressure, strategies and tactics, self-control, group dynamics and relentless training, all compete with the trappings of celebrity and intrusions into personal and domestic life.

When I became a league professional, you basically signed your life away with no going back to the supposedly amateur game.

You were a one-club man unless they wanted or get rid of you or you requested a transfer, which invariably caused all sorts of problems.

Nowadays, in both, rugby is virtually all year round,

there are strictly monitored training regimes, controlled diets, fitness gurus, psychiatrists and so on.

Players have every second of their performance filmed and analysed and are bombarded with game plans and statistics. With the mass of money floating about, there is so much at stake and coverage is so intense and important that nothing can be left to chance.

For top class professionals, their public and private lives are scrutinised and dissected.

Is it good for the game? I am not so sure.

It goes with the territory that for a few of us who inherit the 'mantle of greatness' from our forebears, there is a special benefit and burden.

We do seem to inherit the vital sporting genes that produce instinct, rapid reflex and coordination; the basis of all ball games.

But we also have to learn early on how to handle with good grace the inevitable comment, "you'll never be as good as your dad!"

All of which was a timely reminder for me at the 1985 annual rugby union Varsity match, in which our son John was playing at centre for Oxford.

The dark blues won a knife-edge battle 7-6 in front of a large crowd at Twickenham and we watched proudly as he tackled relentlessly, made a number of good breaks and ran to the point of near-exhaustion.

I noticed, however, that there was something different about his entry in the match day programme.

The normal profile was to name the player, his position, the degree he was reading for and the college he was attending.

To John's embarrassment, his entry alone also added his pedigree, "grandson of Gus, son of Bev".

The same applied to our youngest son Michael when he played for the England Colts in 1987 and now to John's own sons, our grandsons Ben and Luke, who are making their way in school sport with three generations looking over their shoulder. No pressure then!

Sport, as a whole, has changed out of all recognition in my lifetime.

Drug testing, for instance, is now a routine procedure in all and there are fewer places to hide for those who have been using banned substances to enhance their performance, although prescription drug reliance is the next area of concern.

In rugby, there is more coverage and scrutiny than ever of both codes as part of highly lucrative television deals, together with the growing influence of the internet and social media, which gives access to greater information, speculation and opinion than ever before.

The professionalization of players in rugby union in 1995 exposed, at a stroke, the pomposity of entrenched attitudes and prejudices surrounding the protection of amateurism and the consequent vilification of rugby league.

As an illustration, my brother John reminded me: "Bev was director of the Student Rugby League and was short of someone to coach for the Scotland side, so I began my odyssey with them which has lasted until the present day as I am now a very proud president.

"In 1993-4, I organized the first international on home soil against N.E. England at Meadowbank Stadium. There was a lot of controversy over the fixture particularly via the attempted intervention of the Scottish R.U.

"The evening before the game I had a phone call from SRU secretary Bill Hogg telling me that any player taking part in the game would be banned from rugby union.

"That created a dilemma as we had several good union players on the team sheet. Immediately prior to the match I told them of the potential consequences but they unanimously elected to play and the SRU did not attempt to fulfil their threat; it was a big climb-down.

"Fortunately things have changed since then."

Such irrational and defensive attitudes dominated the union game for many years.

Rooted originally in notions of perceived class and superiority it cast a shadow over the game of rugby in both its forms, which has been to the disadvantage of many fine players and the development of the game itself.

More recently, competition between the two versions and unpleasant restrictive practices have had to give way to a growing realisation of similarity and an appreciation of the need for free movement.

With their access to greater finance, sponsorship, investment, player payment, marketing and promotion, union has, even more than players, taken league's coaches for their superior defensive systems and techniques.

There is now talk of a hybrid – I hate that word – version of the sport being trialled in Australia with modified rules drawn up by entrepreneurs.

This distant prospect of merger has not yet attracted sufficient support to proceed, there is no demand from broadcasters – yet, nor for the union club game move to summer.

Both rugby codes in the UK are, effectively, controlled by television finance, not fans or sponsors.

Their media contracts are now a controlling factor as to when, where and what time teams play each other and their need is for subscriptions or licence fees, first and foremost.

Both Sides of the Fence

Non-rugby aficionados globally can see the skills overlap and the potential advantage of having a single, understandable, attractive, summer-based, worldwide game to rival soccer.

It may even be a more coherent view than those who defend their narrow, often vested interest in the status quo, as the general interest in union's Olympic 7s demonstrated, and league attempting to get 9s recognition in the Commonwealth Games.

I have long been convinced that a combination of the best of both rugbys would provide an exceptional spectacle.

The mastery of a wide range of skills both in and out of physical contact provides a much greater array of challenges that can be seen on any soccer pitch.

My view, as someone has always been passionate about both sports, both as a participant and spectator, is that they can be equally magnificent spectacles when played to their best.

But both suffer nowadays due to technicalities in the rules which cause breakdowns in play resulting in too much tackling and kicking and not enough running and handling.

How I long for a concerted attempt to bring both sports together, a merger with a revised set of rules and a single line of management could shake the sporting world.

It seems to me that the time is right for such a proposal, never before have more nations carried an oval ball.

There have already been some attempts to bring the games closer together.

The RFL and RFU have sanctioned cross-code matches after Wigan and Bath met to show off their respective wares in 1996 and Wigan and Bradford entered and, eye-openingly for many, won the Middlesex 7s.

Pressure will eventually come from some sponsor or

a number of political and financial sources to develop a serious feasibility appraisal of this apparent anomaly presented by two versions of the same sport in opposition to one another.

Only rugby is at war with itself.

In traditional areas, fewer youngsters are taking up the game and clubs are fishing in the same, smaller pools and in developing nations, the divide is not seen, rugby is just rugby.

It needs a think tank of various bodies to bring us into the modern sporting world including funders like Sport England, the Department of Culture, Media and Sport, representatives of the media, major sponsors and the players.

History and heritage of each does not have to be ditched. They did, after all, come from the same initial source and the world has moved on, the best of each makes a more than considerable, sustainable whole.

A specific timetable for potential change should be established and trials of 'New Rugby' carried out under a set of common rules bringing together the best features of each, but with promoting entertainment paramount.

The potential for success is limitless, not least in terms of global spread. It is through international fixtures that the revised sport would make the biggest initial impact.

Beyond that, taking the new format into schools should be relatively easy to implement and at club level, both professional and community, the opportunities, challenges and being part of something much bigger would, I believe, outweigh the sacrifices.

In fact, in England it may be easier than first thought to implement because the structure of the leagues in the two codes is remarkably similar.

Both have fully professional elite leagues sitting at the

top of a pyramid of semi-professional and then amateur clubs.

At the pinnacle, as in football, there is a fabulous opportunity for a European competition leading in to a World Club Series, there could even be international promotion and relegation like in the Davis Cup and just imagine what an event a World Cup could be, truly universal.

The barriers to cooperation are being eroded already, players can now cross the great divide almost at will.

Sonny Bill Williams can hardly remember which code he is playing as he trots to-and-fro between one and the other.

Global rugby stars like Ritchie McCaw, Greg Inglis, Brian Habana, Kevin Sinfield, Dan Carter, Israel Folau, Courtney Laws, Sam Burgess, Johnathan Thurston ... are now well known; wouldn't it be magnificent if they were able to cross swords on the same pitch?

Most of the grey areas would involve the restart situation; scrums, line-outs, rucks and mauls and the play the ball.

Some aspects of rugby union are highly technical and often difficult for spectators and viewers to understand, whereas rugby league – with the ball always visible and in play for longer – is easier to appreciate due to simplification of the rules in the physical contact area.

Each has their nuances but a codified set, like in all other sports, makes perfect sense.

With my 60-odd years' experience as a player, coach, administrator and supporter in both camps, and having taken on board soundings from both sides of the fence from people whom I greatly respect and admire, I reckon there is a template for 'New Rugby.'

Teams would be 13-a-side; that provides more space for open play and reduces congestion from around the ruck, maul, scrum and line-out. The scrum would have a 3-2-1-formation to accommodate that.

After the ball had gone into touch, lineouts would be a minimum of three and maximum of six players, which would provide spectacular skills, quicker delivery, less congestion and more opportunity to get the ball into open space.

Points would be five for a try, two for a penalty or conversion and one for a drop goal, placing a greater emphasis on handling than kicking which is what has made so many games, especially in union, sterile.

Adoption of the 40/20 strategic kick from league and a turnover where the ball was kicked from if it goes out of play in the in-goal area.

In addition, I'd advocate no tries to be scored directly from any type of kick, thus creating the need for more passing close to the try-line.

Scrums need to be rethought, the ball should be put in straight down the middle and all contested but with player safety paramount.

A knock-on should be given if the ball is dropped in any direction. That stops uncertainly, with the non-offending side restarting by an option of scrum or play-the-ball.

Stricter penalties for dangerous play such as head-high tackles, kicking, punching and spear-tackling should be adopted, with the sin bin to be retained with different time penalties for varied offences.

I have left the most contentious area to last; ruck and maul or play-the-ball?

The union ruck is an exciting area for many connoisseurs of the game, but is a complete mystery for the casual spectator. It is dynamic and often brutal and causes multiple problems for the referee and often physical danger for the players. The play-the-ball in league – and used by most union clubs in training – is a much simpler operation and less dangerous, but tends to interrupt the flow of play.

There is no easy answer but my own view, after much deliberation, would be to use the limited tackle rule of rugby league.

If the ball is played correctly, it is a much more clear cut operation, easily understood by observers and far less dangerous.

There is no doubt in my mind that, in the fullness of time, the two sports will be as one.

Even with the triumphs I've had on both sides of the fence, I'd love to have played it.

Investigate our other titles and
stay up to date with all our latest releases at
www.scratchingshedpublishing.co.uk